THE
CLOTHING
CARE HANDBOOK

KATHERINE ROBINSON

CONSULTANTS:

Marcia Bayard
Necolya Grigsby Fry
Lara Martina

FAWCETT COLUMBINE ✂ NEW YORK

THE
CLOTHING
CARE HANDBOOK

KATHERINE ROBINSON

CONSULTANTS:

Marcia Bayard
Necolya Grigsby Fry
Lara Martina

FAWCETT COLUMBINE ✄ NEW YORK

**For my children,
Guy and Phoebe Isabel**

Contents

THE CLOTHING CARE HANDBOOK would not have been possible without the help of many people. I especially wish to thank Mary Albert Ellis, doyenne of lace specialists; Helene Von Rosenstiel of Restorations; Kenneth Trommers of J. Press; Mme. Sophie Pourmel of the New York City Ballet and Richard Wagner of the Metropolitan Opera costume departments; Lenny Coleman of Carol Art Cleaners; Fisher Rhymes of The Manmade Fiber Association; Jean Parker of Overland Sheepskin; Lou Rosenberg of Artbag; Susan Smyth of Cricketeer; Victor Canners of Cadillac Shoe Products; Meg Kadlec of The Shoe Service Institute; and Christopher Connolly of The Cluett, Peabody Co.

THE CLOTHING CARE HANDBOOK

KATHERINE ROBINSON

CONSULTANTS:

Marcia Bayard
Necolya Grigsby Fry
Lara Martina

FAWCETT COLUMBINE ✕ NEW YORK

Introduction

Ever since the first cavewoman worried when her fur sarong got wet, people have been dealing with the problems and pleasures of clothing care. Some are concerned about cold storage; others have taught themselves to mend and darn and shirr; all have had to deal with spots, stains, and wrinkles.

Until very recently, the care and preservation of clothing was done entirely at home. Until the 1930s, only natural fibers had to be considered, and clothing care was a traditional domestic science handed down from generation to generation or passed along through books about household management.

Unfortunately much of that traditional know-how no longer applies. Man-made fibers, automatic washers and dryers, steam irons, and new cleaning products all make for new clothes-care dilemmas even while they are making life easier for us by shortening the time we spend in the laundry room.

Hence the need for *The Clothing Care Handbook,* the wardrobe manual with up-to-date answers to *all* your apparel-related questions—everything from how to buy clothes that last and repay the time you put into their care to how to cut dry-cleaning costs and how to store things properly.

You'll find this book easy to use in handling emergencies as well as for browsing and general information gathering. To get a quick answer to a question, consult the Index first. For general information on treating a specific kind of fabric, look it up in Chapter 12, first in the section on fibers, then in the section on fabrics. The Contents pages will help you locate the proper procedures for taking care of your clothes, and the many charts and lists will show you exactly how to proceed and which techniques to use. Everything is cross-indexed for easy reference.

My colleagues and I have researched and described up-to-the-minute changes in labeling laws, fabric care, and clothing maintenance. We hope you'll enjoy the book and use it often, spurred on by the confidence that comes from knowing what to do.

With the high price of clothes, who doesn't need to know how to make them last longer? With our busy lives, who doesn't need time- and energy-saving tips? We no longer live in caves . . . so why go on living in the dark?

Buying Wisely

Care of your clothes can be an unwelcome and some-times overwhelming job, but there are ways to simplify it. The very first step is to buy garments that suit your clothing-care habits and that repay the care you give them.

LOOKING AT YOUR WARDROBE ——————

To assess just how manageable your own wardrobe is, take a look at the clothes you already have and answer the following questions:

- Do you have a lot of easy-care "Machine Wash Warm, Tumble Dry" clothes, or do your garments require in-dividual attention such as handwashing or ironing? If the latter, do you have time to do this? For example, where do you do your laundry? Going out to the laun-dromat makes it tough to deal with clothes needing special care, such as soap instead of detergent or hanging to dry instead of machine drying.
- Do you spend more time ironing than you would like?
- Do most of your clothes look good for years, or do you find that many of them fade and wilt too quickly?

Now review your buying habits:

- Do you look at care labels *before* buying to consider how much and what kind of upkeep they need?
- Do you find yourself returning many articles (or think-ing of returning them) because after washing or dry cleaning they don't look the same?

After you have taken stock of your answers, it will be easier to decide if you want to go for the easy-care clothes—a good idea if you're pressed for time or have to take your laundry out—or if you are the sort of person who enjoys caring for clothes that require special treatment.

Before proceeding to the nitty-gritty of clothes buying, take time out to assess what you already have. You'll definitely have more patience with clothing care if you weed clothes out twice a year—once in the spring and once in the fall. These are the kinds of garments you should consider doing away with:

- Clothes that no longer fit.
- Clothes that no longer respond well to washing or dry cleaning—for instance, that droop or crease easily when folded.
- Clothes that have not been worn *at all* for two years or more. Exceptions: something made of natural fiber (or almost all natural fiber) in excellent condition that fits really well and might conceivably have appeal as a vintage item later—a party dress, a coat, a classically tailored suit.
- Clothes that need costly alterations to be comfortably wearable.

A good guide in choosing your wardrobe is to look at which clothes have become old favorites, worn again and again, and which have not. You will probably find that those that *look* good also *wear* well: they don't have to be washed after every wearing, can be touched up with a little steam ironing, and have held their original shape and color through many washings or dry cleanings.

The plain fact is that well-made clothes really repay the effort of caring for them. A workable wardrobe that suits your figure, style, and way of life as well as your purse is much less of a trial to care for. So

- *Don't* snap up something just because it's on sale or because it's the latest thing. Impulse buying should be confined to clothes that fit in with what you already have and that don't require costly care or alterations (more than moving a button or taking up a hem). Be tough—it's amazing how many things lose their glamour the moment you take off the price tag.
- *Don't*, on the whole, buy things that won't go with your existing wardrobe, both in style and—above all—in color. Unless you are an indefatigable shopper, the

irritation and expense of having to go out and buy the other things that complete the look or color scheme will far outweigh the fun of having something new.

- *Do* know your own colors and the kinds of clothes you feel really comfortable in. Some people are the dressy type and wouldn't go out without stockings, heels, and jewelry. Others spend most of their days in trousers and shirts. Sticking to your own style, whatever it is, simplifies clothing care because similar clothes usually require similar care. Coordinating colors makes care easier because you don't find yourself rushing to dry-clean the navy skirt that is the only thing that goes with your fuchsia blouse.

BUYING WELL-MADE CLOTHES ———

Some general statements can be made about the "good buy," but you should learn to evaluate each item on its own. All the elements that go into making a garment are important—the yarn, weaving or knitting, dyeing, finishing, design, and workmanship—but the way everything *works together* is, too. Experience will of course give you the feel of quality as well.

Be aware that names today aren't what they used to be, despite the advertising blitz. Mass merchandising of designer clothes has devalued the term, probably for good. The words "designer" and "couture" (beautifully designed and mostly handmade clothes) used to be synonymous but are no longer, so don't take anything at face value. Instead, carefully inspect everything you buy, inside and out.

For quality performance, consider the following:

- The clothing industry estimates only fifty or so wearings for clothes in easy-care man-made fabrics. Clothes in a good natural-fiber fabric (which may contain a small percentage of man-made fiber) should last much longer. To calculate which is the better bargain, divide the price of the item by the number of wearings *you* expect to get from it.
- Depending on the article of clothing, the material should be one that can easily be altered. Can you let out a seam without ruining the garment? Permanent press, acetates, acrylic, and modacrylic are difficult if not impossible to alter, while cotton, linen, and wool take kindly to alterations.

When shopping, dress in easy-to-get-out-of clothes. Don't wear barrettes or other hair ornaments that can hook into clothes. Keep makeup minimal. (This goes for the daily dressing ritual as well. Add the barrettes and makeup *after* the clothes are on!)

- There should be a hem allowance (on sleeves, too), especially in children's clothes. European clothes are often made with alterations, or at least children's growth, in mind—but be sure to allow for a full size of shrinkage if the items are cotton.
- The fabric should be compatible with the design. If the material isn't very resilient (i.e., silk, linen, rayon, and the acetates and acrylics), the clothes must fit freely enough so there won't be strain on seams and fabric. Tight silk pants, for instance, tend to fray and split, while a more flowing cut can last for years.
- There should be *no* telltale signs of poor or shoddy design, such as
  — awkward hip measurements that show up in pockets that bulge, "whiskers" fanning out from the crotch, and back seams that show strain at the waistline.
  — misplaced gathers or pleats that cause strain on fabric and ride up when worn.
  — collar and shoulders that drag backward, creating a gap at the back of the neck and a pull on front buttons.
  — unreinforced stress points such as corners of pockets or the shoulder seam of knits.
- There should be no telltale signs of poor workmanship. Along with bad design, poor workmanship is the main reason some clothes already look tired on the rack. This can't be remedied at home and makes caring for the item doubly difficult. So don't buy something (with hopes of home repair) if you notice
  — puckering along seams or trim such as piping or binding (slight puckering of some inexpensive synthetics seems to be common these days, but it shouldn't be).
  — knits that aren't elastic, especially at ribbing, or that don't shed wrinkles—smooth out when patted—immediately.
  — bunching of fabric because bulky excess material hasn't been removed, particularly at corners.
  — missing or broken stitches.
  — marks in pile fabric and discolorations on synthetics.
  — shine on matte fabrics.
  — creases that aren't straight and properly positioned.

— uneven hemlines.

— a fabric weave that does not go straight up and down . . . unless the garment is deliberately cut on the bias.

— limp or unnaturally stiff or clinging fabric.

— side seams that aren't straight up and down.

— zippers that don't lie flat.

— shoulder seams that aren't on the natural shoulder-line.

— bagging in the front of pants and skirts, cling under the rear, or a gap at the waist. (If the store has a tailor/seamstress you can have the waist pinned to see if an alteration is simple and practical and either have them do it or leave the pins in so you can.)

— poorly pressed tailored clothes. Proper pressing must be done by the manufacturer, and done meticulously, since this gives clothes their proper fit and guides all later pressing.

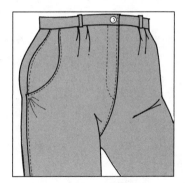

KNOWING QUALITY FABRICS ——————

It *is* important both for looks and durability to choose clothes made with good fabric. One excellent way to learn about fabric performance is to look at samples in a fabric shop or dry goods department with a wide range of materials. Pick a category—for example, silk crepe de chine or even plain white cotton—find a knowledgeable salesperson, and ask to be shown samples in that category so you can compare them. Start with the top of the line and work down, or vice versa. Use sight, touch, and even smell to assess the fabrics. An intuitive sense that something is a good value will come in time, but here are some basic tips and tests to help you along the way:

• The manufacturer is responsible for stabilizing color, size, and finish so that the fabric only gradually loses its original character. Return items that show a dramatic change after the first washing or two. (See "Many Happy Returns," below, if you find yourself in this fix.)

• To identify skilled weaving, knitting, or finishing, take a handful of fabric and squeeze it (except for intentionally stiffened materials like linen, organdy, taffeta, and organza). If you squeeze about ten seconds and re-

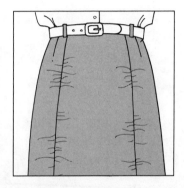

lease, then smooth with your hand, wrinkles should disappear right away or in a matter of minutes.

- Avoid scratchy materials. The feel of the cloth should be good *of its kind:* a soft silk should have a creamy, fluid hang; a wool should feel springy. There is no good reason for abrasive quality, except in rough tweeds (check these and all stiff fabrics to be sure they are lined).

- Natural materials in particular should smell fresh. Permanent press should have no fishy or off odor. Give the article in question a good sniff before buying.

- In natural fabrics, select heavier weights for durability. If you search out 16-ounce denim (sometimes called workweight denim or megadenim) you'll get a much longer-wearing pair of jeans. A thick cotton knit or terrycloth will give you more wear than more loosely knit material using finer yarns. For hard wear, even nylon fabric (in clothes and luggage, for instance) should be a 2-ounce weight (or more) for real strength. Look for this information on the tag or ask the salesperson.

- When buying blends, pick those that draw on the virtues of each of the fibers used. If you like the feel, look, and other strengths of natural fibers, go for blends that include up to 25 percent of man-made material. These fibers add durability while lowering the cost.

- Whenever possible buy cottons that are preshrunk and colorfast. The words "combed cotton" on a label ensure that you are getting a smoother, stronger, more easily ironed fabric. Mercerized cotton is similarly improved. The salesperson should be able to tell you when cotton is colorfast.

- Test the tension in knits. Stretch and release to check elasticity, then bunch, release, and smooth out to check wrinkle resistance.

- Avoid the following bad bets for long wear unless you're buying just for fun. These are the styles or fabrics that don't wash and/or dry clean well:
  — acetate pile.
  — acrylic knits.
  — Angora rabbit hair (alone or in blends).
  — bouclé, chenille, and other nubbies, especially man-mades.
  — handpainted clothing and those with surface printing.
  — glued-on flocking or designs.

For a no-iron wardrobe that's elegant, try silk-like acetates and polyesters, knits of all kinds (if top quality) and the dry-cleanable worsted wools and wool and wool-silk blends. For evening, try all the washable silks in colors—honan, pongee, surah, shantung, silk linen.

- novelty knits containing metal, ribbon, feathers, mixed yarns, etc.
- soft leather clothes and trim as well as imitation suede.
- pleats in natural fibers, rayon, and acetate. They aren't permanently set. Dry cleaning can be tricky, since it's hard to get proper pressing today.
- rayon challis and other very soft or sheer rayons.
- whites that must be dry cleaned. They require extra care that many cleaners don't give them to keep them from turning gray.
- elastic in clothes that must be dry cleaned. Solvent breaks it down quickly.

NOTE: Fragile materials like silk moiré and chiffon are not included on this list since they are only meant to be worn occasionally.

Quality, it should be noted, is not necessarily synonymous with price. Certain inexpensive items—standard brands of cotton underwear, for example—are good quality for their intended use. They are made of the proper fabric for something that is worn next to the skin and that must be washed often. They are constructed properly—knitted—for something that must stretch and give a lot during wear. They are durable, with heavy-duty elastic webbing and overlapped seams tacked down at points of stress, so they will stand up to frequent wear. For the price, they are actually very good quality. Some others: Shetland wool sweaters, corduroy skirts and trousers, and all-cotton tailored shirts.

Much more expensive items—especially in a new style whose construction hasn't been thought through carefully—can easily fall apart in half the time. Look for good fabric, good design, and good workmanship *before* looking at the price tag.

MANY HAPPY RETURNS ────────────

Clothes are made by human hands—usually many pairs of them, in fact—so there are bound to be surprises even when you buy a familiar label. Don't be afraid to return a garment that doesn't work. Consider returns a normal part of buying clothes; stores certainly do. If possible, shop at stores that have a generous, hassle-free returns policy.

Even after one or two washings or cleanings, *if* you

have followed instructions to the letter, take the clothes back if they fade, shrink dramatically, or lose their shape, or if the fabric goes limp and lifeless. Take them back also when the problem is pilling, puckering, or off-kilter seams. Whatever the reason, a return is made easier if you ask about the store's policy before you buy and keep the sales slip handy, at least until after the first few washings or cleanings.

Remember that even sale, "special purchase," and "not returnable" items often *can* be returned if they exhibit the kind of major defect we're talking about.

You will have better luck returning unsatisfactory items if you're a regular customer and if the store is a large, established one. Be sure you have the receipt, package the clothes neatly, and be certain that you have followed care-label instructions carefully. Take the package first to the department where you bought the garment. Usually there is a service desk nearby; if not, the sales staff will refer you to the proper person.

If you are asked to send the clothes back to the manufacturer—more likely in smaller stores—be sure to take out some insurance on them and then keep the mailing form and a copy of your letter stating your complaint and what you want done about it. Follow up, by phone or letter, if you get no reply in a month or six weeks.

Whereas stores give credit on a return, a manufacturer will have to find a suitable replacement. Have patience; this can be difficult, since the clothes you bought were made at least three and perhaps six months before you bought them. (Clothes bought on sale will have been around even longer.)

BUYING BY MAIL ████████████

This may now be America's most popular way of shopping. While mail-order shopping is convenient, sometimes saves money, and may offer clothes that can't be found in local stores, problems do arise. To avoid them, keep the following facts in mind:

1. You're *seeing* a sample, not *handling* it. Think carefully about possible problems with fit, color, fabric, and even texture.
2. A good buy is one you know how to care for. Before you invest, call the tool-free number listed and ask what care is required if the catalogue doesn't tell you.

3. You can also call the toll-free number if you're unsure about any of the following:
   —sizing—have your measurements ready.
   —the fabric type—napped or smooth, loosely woven or firm like a twill, preshrunk or not if it's cotton—or fiber content.
   —the length.
   —the size of the hem allowance and the kind of hem.
   —match-up between the color in the photograph and that of the original.
   —type of cuffs (especially whether they are elasticized or not).
4. The photograph is supposed to *add* to the information in the blurb, so be wary of buying something that isn't shown face on or at least with the model in a natural pose. A dramatic or distorted pose can be used to hide poor design.

Mail-order returns should be trouble-free. Check the following list when you order. Then keep everything in a convenient file.

- *Find out the returns policy before you buy.* You may prefer to deal only with companies that make check (cash) returns.
- Print or type clearly and go over all order entries carefully; missing information is the most frequent cause of mix-ups. *Always* keep the catalogue with a copy of your original order and the company's address and phone number. You will need them in case of a delay or return.
- Keep a record of the return itself, including a copy of the invoice and dated copies of any accompanying letters and the insurance and postage receipts. You will need them if the parcel goes astray or if you do not hear from the company within approximately thirty days.
- If you do not get reimbursement or credit by then, write the company Customer Service Department explaining the problem (keep a copy of your letter) and enclose a copy of your order, a copy of your canceled check or credit-card billing, and a copy of the dated insurance slip from the post office. *Never send originals.*
- If you still hear nothing, after thirty days contact Mail Order Action Line, Direct Mail Association, 6 East

43rd Street, New York, NY 10017. Send them a covering letter describing the problem; enclose copies of all your backup material, including the check or credit-card billing, and ask them to intervene. It can take time, but they successfully resolve most problems.

Shopping can be wonderful fun. Doing it right so that clothes reward the time you spend in caring for them will make your wardrobe much more of a pleasure to you.

CHAPTER TWO

Out, Damned Spot!

You finish cooking the spaghetti sauce, lick the spoon, and dribble sauce on your new silk shirt. What can you do? The first and most important step in stain removal is *not to panic*. Most situations aren't disastrous if you learn and remember the emergency measures below, keep the necessary supplies and equipment ready and easily available, and keep in mind the "Cardinal Rules of Stain Removal" (see page 16).

EMERGENCY MEASURES

Do these immediately with any stain:
- Scrape off any loose surface matter.
- Blot up as much liquid (if any) as possible with an absorbent cloth such as a napkin—go on blotting for several minutes, using fresh cloths as needed. (Use paper napkins only if nothing else is available, since they leave lint.)
- If the stain is plain grease, such as bacon fat, dust it with plain talcum powder or cornstarch if there is some on hand.
- If the stain is not greasy, flush the area with a tablespoon of room-temperature water* *if* the clothes are washable or on the following short list of "dry clean only" fabrics: silk broadcloth, linen weave, honan, pongee, surah or crepe de chine (a smooth crepe—*do not*

*Never use hot water on stains at this point.

wet pebbly or other textured crepes); silk blended with a washable fiber; wool tweeds, flat weaves and knits; rayon; and fabrics of washable fibers labeled "Dry Clean" simply because the *construction* of the garment requires dry cleaning (a pleated cotton dress, or tailored suit, for example).

Rinsing with water dilutes the stain and removes at least some of it while it's still fresh, minimizing the damage it can do and the work you must do later. For successful results, however, you should complete stain removal as indicated on the chart on pp. 24 as soon as possible—preferably within a day or two.

Here are the stains that should be rinsed out promptly:

Acids, such as vinegar and lemon juice

Alcoholic beverages (including beer, wine and liqueurs)

Blood

Caramel sauce, syrup

Catsup

Caviar

Cereals, cooked and dry

Cider

Chlorine bleach

Cream

Cream rinse for hair

Curry sauce

Depilatories

Egg, eggnog

Food coloring

Fruit juices

Gravy, meat juices

Hand lotion

Honey

Jam

Jello

Metal polish

Metal tarnish

Milk, ice cream, condensed milk

Mouthwash

Rennet (junket) custards

Soft drinks

Starches, such as dough

Sugar, syrups

Tea

Tobacco, nicotine

Tomato juice

Toothpaste

Typewriter correction fluid (if bottle says water-base)

Urine

Vegetable stains

WHAT YOU NEED _____

Most of the cleaning agents and equipment you need for proper stain removal will be familiar. All can be found at your supermarket, drugstore, or hardware store.

The list is not as formidable as you might think. Only the starred items are absolutely necessary; the other items are for use in the kinds of situations most of us turn over to the dry cleaner. And everything fits easily on one shelf.

- a teaspoon.*
- white blotting paper.*
- absorbent cotton cloths such as cheesecloth (especially for textured fabrics) or tea towels.*
- chamois cloth.
- two or three capped plastic squeeze bottles.*
- small cellulose or foam sponges.*
- enamel, glass, or china bowls in several sizes.*
- sink or bucket for soaking.*
- medium-soft flat-bristle toothbrush.*
- 3-to-4-inch-long flat-cut nailbrush.*

- tall, 2½-gallon enamel pot.*

- plant mister.
- hairdryer.
- *Absorbent powders* for soaking up oil and grease: *French (tailor's marking) chalk, cornstarch, or plain (noncosmetic) talcum powder.
- *lubricants* for releasing organic stains such as fruit juice: *Glycerin, amyl acetate (banana oil), or coconut oil.
- *catalysts/enzymes* for breaking down protein: *Enzyme pre-soak powders or "detergent boosters" such as Axion or Biz.
- *solvents* for dissolving grease and oil:
  For washables only:
  * laundry bar soap such as Fels-Naptha, Octagon, or Kirkman.
  * a liquid hard-surface household cleaner, such as Lestoil labeled for use on clothes.
  * household ammonia, plain white vinegar, rubbing alcohol, distilled water, pure acetone (not nail-polish remover).
  For either "Dry Clean Only" or washables: dry-cleaning fluid of the trichloroethane or trichloroethylene type such as Difficult Stain Remover.
- *detergents* for dissolving water-based stains: *Clear or white liquid dishwashing detergent (it can be combined with solvents or lubricants). * liquid heavy-duty laundry detergent.
- *color removers* for bleaching out color after the rest of the stain is gone: * Chlorine bleach or packaged color remover.

Red or white wine: Blot up immediately with an absorbent material—preferably linen. Put a napkin *under* the stain if possible while you blot. *Keep blotting* for several minutes, changing the pad once or twice. Now, if the material with the stain in it is washable, squeeze a little water through the stain, again with a pad underneath if possible, and blot until the area begins to feel dry. If the clothes are "Dry Clean Only," just blot until as dry as possible and mark the area to show the dry cleaner later.

SAFETY PRECAUTIONS ────────

Almost all stain-removal agents are caustic and irritating to the skin. Many are flammable, poisonous, or produce toxic fumes. The dry-cleaning solvent we recommend is *not* flammable, but fumes can be toxic if you have had anything alcoholic to drink. Take these precautions:

- Store in a cool, dry place away from light.
- Don't use near open flame. Don't smoke or drink while working, and turn off nearby electrical appliances (except lights) when using cleaning fluid.
- Work in a well-ventilated spot. Try to have fumes blow *away* from you.
- Don't wash or dry the item by machine until the dry-cleaning fluid has had a chance to evaporate.
- To protect sensitive skin, wear rubber gloves.
- Don't mix your own "recipes" and *never mix* ammonia and chlorine bleach.
- When mixing a solution, pour the water or least harmful liquid into the stronger one—splashes will be the harmless liquid.
- Some of the chemicals used in stain removal react with metal; thus nonmetal containers are suggested. However, plastic containers cannot be used for amyl acetate.

CARDINAL RULES OF STAIN REMOVAL ──────────

1. Do a washability test before spot cleaning if you have any doubts about whether the fabric is colorfast or won't react well to washing.

   Step 1: Test each color for fastness by saturating a small hidden section (perhaps a seam allowance) with a few drops of mild soapsuds. It's easiest to see results if the fabric is placed on an absorbent towel. After a minute or so, blot firmly with a cotton swab or the corner of a towel to see if the color comes off. Check the towel underneath, too. Rinse carefully with a few teaspoons of clear water and blot dry.

Step 2: Now check to see that the fabric won't stretch or shrink out of shape in washing. First look it up in the fabric guide in Chapter 12 to be sure that water won't damage the surface finish. Submerge a cuff or a section of hem for a minute or two in water, squeeze out gently but firmly, and compare with the dry fabric. If it looks basically unchanged, you should be able to spot-clean and wash without any trouble.

Step 3: If you plan to wash the clothes after spot cleaning them, be sure the overall garment construction permits it. Even if the fiber and fabric are washable, the garment itself may not be. For guidelines, see p. 80 in Chapter 5.

2. Deal with stains promptly. Give the problem your undivided attention before the spill or mark dries. Many substances—for example, blood, wine, protein, and paint—change chemically when they dry out. If you can't do the whole job right away, at least perform the emergency measures.

3. Be sure to examine clothes in a good light immediately after wearing them. Many stains become difficult if not impossible to remove if they are washed in hot water or exposed to laundry detergents.

4. Keep equipment clean, handy, and ready for use near a work space: a clean, *well-lighted* surface such as glass, formica, stainless steel, or ceramic tile, none of which react with cleaning chemicals, will do nicely.

5. Except for the emergency treatments mentioned at the beginning of this chapter, items labeled "Dry Clean Only" should be dealt with only by the dry cleaner. He should have a specialist called a spotter to do this work—and if your dry cleaner doesn't, find one who does. If you bring in an item with a stain, tell the cleaner what you think the stain is and, if you've tried to remove it, what you did. (If you *send* clothes in, pin a note to the stain.)

6. Don't scrub, wring, or otherwise treat fabric roughly unless it is tough, like a denim or heavyweight ny-

While most clothes are colorfast—that is, the dye is not released during washing—colors will fade gradually when they are subjected to machine washing in hot water (particularly if the clothes are crowded in) with strong detergents or bleach, or are left to dry in direct sun or are ironed on high heat. To keep colors bright and fresh, use gentle washing methods, presoak clothes rather than bleaching them to get out heavy dirt, and iron them on the back of the fabric when possible. NOTE: **It is quite normal for dark or bright colors—reds, purples and blues predominantly—to bleed surface dye residues during the first four or five launderings even though they are colorfast. Watch for labels warning "Wash Separately." In Europe look for the symbol meaning "wash separately the first four times."**

Travelers, be prepared! Keep a small vial of cornstarch in your purse to dust on oil/grease spills. Also put in your suitcase a small vial or squeeze bottle of 2 tablespoons of liquid dishwashing detergent mixed with ¼ teaspoon of glycerin to wash out water-based stains such as fruit juice, sugar, starch, and washable ink—if the fabric is washable.

lon. Gentle rubbing or brushing of even durable fabrics is best. If you are using a brush, pick one with medium-soft bristles. It's easy to snag yarns of loosely woven or knit fabrics or to disarrange the yarns of delicate fabrics, so you might want to leave these to the pros until you're an old hand at stain removal.

7. Except when bleaching, avoid heat of any kind until you know the stain is coming out.

8. Go slowly until you get used to a technique and find out how a fabric behaves. Use only small amounts of stain remover, testing first on a seam allowance or facing to be sure the agent doesn't cause color to bleed. If dye does start to bleed, STOP AND RINSE IMMEDIATELY WITH WATER, UNLESS YOU'RE USING CLEANING FLUID. (If you are using cleaning fluid, simply evaporate the fluid by waving the garment briskly for a few minutes.)

9. Remove all residues of cleaning agents with a thorough rinsing or, in the case of cleaning fluid, a good airing. Chemicals left to sit can do damage to dyes and fabrics.

10. Patient repetition of a method is often the secret of success. For example, if a stain is getting lighter as you tamp in solvent, keep tamping and adding fresh solvent until no more stain is evident.

11. Because finishes on fabrics differ—and new ones are occasionally introduced—the method suggested for a stain may not work. In that case, a little experimentation may be in order. But whether you use a method given here or try a tip you find elsewhere—hair spray on ink from a ballpoint pen, for example—review the fiber and fabric guides first and then check the index under the name of the item (hats or belts, for instance).

Let's say you want to try hair spray on ballpoint pen ink. You *can* on cotton because the alcohol in hair spray won't damage that fiber; you *can't* on acetate, because it will.

No matter what method you try, remember to rinse (and, with washable clothes, wash) after the treatment.

12. If a procedure works, write it down in your household book so you know exactly what to do the next time.

BASIC STAIN-REMOVING TECHNIQUES ▬▬▬▬▬▬

Removing any stain involves applying one or more cleaning agents with the appropriate technique. Since delicate fabrics cannot be treated the same way as ordinary washables, the stain chart gives separate instructions for each category; be sure to consult the chart before you begin.

Scraping: Scrape off solid matter with a smooth implement like a round teaspoon, dry cloth, or small brush—even a toothbrush. Never use your hand. Let mud, sand, mildew, and other substances that become crumbly when dry, *dry* first, then brush them off.

Blotting and Tamping: Blot up as much of liquid spills as possible with clean absorbent cloths or blotting paper. Sandwich the stain between two absorbent materials if you can. Tamp with the top cloth, lift, and press down again, changing the cloth as soon as it seems saturated. Continue until the garment feels fairly dry. Tamping contains the stain, keeping it from spreading.

Absorbing: Sprinkle absorbent powder evenly on the fresh stain. (You can use powder on any stain you think has oil content.) The powder becomes gummy as it soaks up the stain. After a few minutes, scrape it off gently into your hand with a spoon. Continue reapplying fresh powder and scraping it off until it no longer seems to be absorbing. Leave the last coat on overnight if it's convenient. Brush or vacuum gently before using any recommended further step. If all the powder can't be removed, take the item to the dry cleaner.

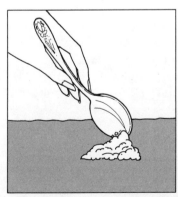

SCRAPING

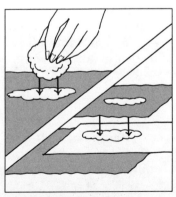

BLOTTING AND TAMPING

ABSORBING

Rinsing: Rinse with cool or lukewarm water to get rid of water-based stains. Work from the back of the fabric *where possible* to keep the stain from working its way deeper into the material, putting an absorbent pad underneath the stained area. Then tamp up the liquid with an absorbent cloth, working across the stain first in one direction, then in the other, to avoid rings.

Using Dry-Cleaning Solvent: Sponge on a little cleaning fluid at a time. If the chart directs you to rinse first, be sure to wait for the fabric to dry before beginning this step. Apply sparingly with a soft, clean cloth or small sponge.

- Again, use an absorbent pad underneath the stain.
- Tamp with an absorbent cloth evenly out from the center of the stain to disperse it, *unless* the stain contains color, such as lipstick or foundation. This feathering-out motion prevents rings. To contain lipstick or other color, simply tamp up and down, taking extra care to change the cleaning cloth often.
- After flushing the stain with cleaning fluid, you can further loosen stubborn spots by sandwiching the stain between pads moistened with

  2 teaspoons cleaning fluid
  ¼ teaspoon coconut oil

Let stand five minutes, then feather out with a fresh pad of absorbent cloth dipped in *plain* cleaning fluid until the mark disappears. It's usually a good idea to feather out all the way to a seam to avoid leaving a ring.

Lubricating: Use an appropriate lubricant to release the stain. Glycerin, coconut oil, and amyl acetate loosen and thus aid in releasing many kinds of stains, though amyl acetate should not be used on acetate/triacetate or rayon.

- Mix the following solution for a spot remover that both lubricates and dissolves washable stains. Keep it in a squeeze bottle with a cap.

  1 tablespoon glycerin or coconut oil, or 1 teaspoon amyl acetate
  1 tablespoon liquid dishwashing detergent
  8 tablespoons water
  Shake before each use.

- Apply the lubricant or lubricant solution lightly. Leave five minutes or so, longer if the stain is old. Keep a pad underneath to collect stain that has been released, or

Grease does dissolve grease, as the old saying goes, but don't use lard, as was once suggested. Instead, use a few drops of amyl acetate (banana oil) or coconut oil in mild suds to saturate the stain before laundering.

sandwich the area between two pads moistened with the solution.

- If the fabric isn't delicate, you can tamp in the lubricant gently with a soft brush or sponge to help dislodge the stain.
- If necessary, repeat the lubricating process several times, using fresh pads and solution.
- Rinse thoroughly with water.

Enzyme Action: An enzyme presoak breaks down proteins and can affect dyes, so test a little of the powder—made into a paste with water—on a hidden area first. If the fabric isn't affected, make more paste with warm water and apply it to the stain. Keep a damp cloth pad on the area and check after half an hour to see if progress is being made. If not, repeat, leaving the paste on for up to twelve hours.

- Enzymes *can* be used on wool and other animal hair, but only briefly—say 10 minutes. Watch carefully.
- Rinse carefully.
- For sturdy washables, make a solution of 2 tablespoons of presoak per 2 gallons of warm water and leave for several hours or overnight to soak.

Laundry Solvents: The most familiar solvent is plain water. Distilled water is best.

- As solvents can dissolve dyes, test a few drops on a hidden area first.
- Apply as for lubricants.
- If the stain is oil-based, the chart will suggest bar soap or hard-surface household cleaner. A prewash spray used just before laundering is fine if you're *sure* the stain won't set. *Your best bet is to hand-remove a stain before regular laundering.* For delicates, a rubbing alcohol/water solution is preferred. Dilute rubbing alcohol with 2 parts water to 1 part alcohol to add to soap and water. This is also useful for removing colored stains. Keep alcohol-water solution in a labeled plastic bottle.
- *For simple nonoily stains* on any washable fabric *except* washable wool, animal hair, silk, spandex, and acetate/triacetate, you will probably be successful with either bar soap or a mixture of
    1 teaspoon of household ammonia
    1 teaspoon of liquid dishwashing soap/detergent
    1 teaspoon of water

When you're nearly sideswiped on one of those days when the gutters are awash with muddy slush, go ahead and stamp your feet in outrage. It's amazing how much of the offending muck will come off. *Don't brush the remaining dirt off until it has dried!*

kept in a plastic squeeze bottle with a cap. Shake before each use. Work into the spot, let sit a few minutes, then wash out with water, rinsing until the water runs clear.

Bleaching: This is what is called a reducing process, which means it burns off (oxidizes) surface material such as tannin in wine, mustard, and other stains rather than simply dissolving them. Bleaching weakens cloth fibers to some degree, which is why it is a last resort. For an all-over whitening, as when something has gone pink from picking up color in the washing machine, *color remover,* which is not a bleach, is more effective and gentler. Chlorine bleach, of course, affects colors, even beige and off-white, which is why it's risky to spot-bleach unless you are dealing with a pure white linen or cotton. Not only should chlorine bleach *not* be used on wool, other animal hair, silk, spandex, acetate/triacetate, and nonfast colors, but it is also harmful to no-iron fabrics, including no-iron cotton.

- To use chlorine bleach to remove stains, make a solution of
  ⅓ cup of chlorine bleach
  2 gallons of water—the hottest the fabric will stand
  in a *nonmetal container.* Note: This is a much stronger solution than that used in washing machines.
- The bleaching process takes only 3 or 4 minutes, although you can let whites steep longer in a milder solution. Be sure the clothes float freely and keep stirring them.
- Neutralize after bleaching by adding several tablespoons of white vinegar to the rinse water. Rinse meticulously because any bleach residue will age, yellow, and burn fabric. NOTE: If you spill chlorine bleach on something, rinse it immediately with a half vinegar/half water solution, then plenty of plain water.
- If you must spot-bleach a print or white, be sure the material is colorfast and *dry.* Make a mild solution of ½ teaspoon of bleach and 4 tablespoons of water, stir well, and apply a few *drops* to the area. Watch to see when it has taken effect—1 to 2 minutes usually—then

flush liberally with vinegar/water as above and launder. (For an old-fashioned but still useful method of spot bleaching with lemon juice, see p. 49.)

HOW TO USE THE STAIN CHART

- Identify the fiber and the fabric of your stained garment, consulting the fiber and fabric guides in Chapter 12 as necessary. Even if you know that the *fiber* is treatable, double-check the fabric guide to be sure the fabric is safe to treat at home.
- Clothes are either general washables or tricky items. Decide which yours is.

General washables include all machine-washables and cotton, linen, and man-made handwashables that are *colorfast.*

Tricky items include handwashable wool and other animal hair, silk, rayon, acetate, and triacetate, again provided they test colorfast and the particular *fabric* can safely be spot cleaned. If you customarily handwash something labeled "Dry Clean Only," you *can* use water-based stain removers. But if the stain calls for dry-cleaning fluid, take stains to the dry cleaner.

- Identify the stain.
- Follow special information instructions where they are given.
- Follow steps (in order) as indicated, using the techniques and solutions (lubricant, neutralizer, enzyme paste, etc.) described earlier in this chapter. Once the stain is gone, you need not do any further steps even though they are given under the method. As the chart indicates, some but not all of these methods are needed when you tackle any stain. The agent used in each step depends on what the stain is *and* whether or not the agent is safe on the fiber used in the fabric.
- If the stain in question is not on this list, take the garment immediately to the dry cleaner. If you try one of these methods and it does not work, take the item directly to a good cleaner and explain what you did.
- On tricky items, use only mild cleaning agents—no ammonia, no regular detergents, no hard-surface liquid cleaner, no acetone, no chlorine bleach—and use only small amounts.

How to tell what hit you: Most water-soluble stains bead up for a few seconds before being absorbed into the cloth. They may dry a little stiff. Oily ones don't. Stains with sugar or starch content may dry whitish and/or stiff or show a white mark when scratched. Oils characteristically show up as darker patches completely absorbed into the cloth. See "Unknown Stains" on page 50 for how to get out stains that remain a mystery.

THE STAIN CHART

	GENERAL WASHABLES		TRICKY ITEMS	
STAIN	SPECIAL INFORMATION	STEPS	SPECIAL INFORMATION	STEPS
Acids (vinegar, lemon juice, etc.)	To neutralize: Saturate with a solution of 1 part ammonia to 8 parts water.	● Rinse. ● Neutralize. ● Rinse again. ● Wash immediately or blot dry and wash later.	To neutralize: Saturate with a few drops of a solution of 16 parts water, 1 part ammonia.	● Rinse. ● Neutralize. ● Rinse again (very carefully). ● Blot to dry unless washing immediately. *Act fast:* acids can do permanent damage quickly.
Adhesive (glue, paste)	Take to the dry cleaner if there's a lot or if it has set.	● Harden with ice. ● Pick off what you can. ● Apply dry-cleaning solvent. ● Apply lubricant solution. ● Dry. If necessary, repeat all steps. ● Wash.	Take to the dry cleaner.	
Alcoholic Beverages (wine, spirits, liqueurs)		● Rinse. ● Let table and bed linens soak in mild detergent solution overnight. ● Apply lubricant solution, with one tablespoon of vinegar added. ● Wash. ● Bleach, if necessary.	Treat promptly.	● Rinse. ● Apply lubricant solution. If no improvement, take to cleaner.

GENERAL WASHABLES			TRICKY ITEMS	
STAIN	SPECIAL INFORMATION	STEPS	SPECIAL INFORMATION	STEPS
Ammonia	To neutralize: Saturate with a few drops of 2 parts water, 1 part vinegar.	● Rinse. ● Neutralize. ● Rinse. ● Blot to dry unless washing immediately. *Act fast:* alkalis can do permanent damage quickly.	Neutralize as for general washables. Best to take wool, silk, good clothes to the dry cleaner after rinsing.	● Rinse. ● Neutralize. ● Rinse very carefully. ● Wash immediately or blot dry and wash later. ● Rinse. ● Wash as usual, or take to the dry cleaner.
Animal Slobber	Protein, sometimes with plant material. Never use heat in removing. Take silk and wool to the dry cleaner.	● Rinse in warm water. ● Flush briefly with solution of 1 part ammonia to 3 parts water. ● Rinse. ● Apply enzyme paste for a half hour. ● Wash. If color remains, flush with alcohol-water solution. ● Rinse.	Take silk and wool to the dry cleaner.	● Rinse in lukewarm water. ● Flush with ammonia solution. ● Rinse. ● Continue as for general washables.
Baby Food/ Formula	Extra careful rinsing and use of enzymes prevents yellow stains from developing later.	● Rinse. Use enzyme paste. ● Wash in detergent suited to fabric. ● Repeat.	Use enzymes as for regular washables, except on silk. Use cautiously on wool. Best to take wool, silk, good clothes to the dry cleaner after rinsing.	● Rinse. ● Use enzyme paste cautiously. ● Rinse. ● Repeat if working and fabric is not affected. ● Wash as usual, or take to the dry cleaner.

GENERAL WASHABLES			TRICKY ITEMS	
STAIN	SPECIAL INFORMATION	STEPS	SPECIAL INFORMATION	STEPS
Beer (*see* Alcoholic Beverages)	Old stains may need an application of enzyme paste before washing.			
Beets and Berries	Be sure to scrape all surface matter off. Rinse cotton and linen with hot water—pouring it through from 18 inches above taut fabric is a good idea.	• Rinse. Apply lubricant solution. • Use enzyme paste if stain is stubborn. • Wash. • Bleach as necessary.	Be sure to scrape any surface matter off.	• Rinse. • Proceed as for regular washables, but wash with mild detergent. • If colorfast, use alcohol (solvent) solution on remaining color. Do not use chlorine bleach. • Take stubborn stain to the dry cleaner.
Blood	Treat fresh if at all possible. Rinse with cold water even if remaining steps must wait.	• Rinse. Apply lubricant solution with ¼ teaspoon of ammonia added. Rinse after 15 minutes. • Use enzyme paste. • Wash in soap or detergent. If residue, soak in 2 tablespoons of enzyme presoak to 2 quarts of water, 8 hours or overnight.	Treat fresh. Do not use enzyme paste on silk.	• Rinse. • Use enzyme paste cautiously. • Rinse. • Wash as usual or take to the dry cleaner.
Butter/ Margarine	Treat immediately.	• Use absorbent powder *unless* you can promptly use bar soap or hard-surface cleaner.	Take to cleaner unless cotton, linen, spandex, nylon, or polyester *handwashable*.	• Use absorbent powder on fresh stain. Use bar soap. • Apply lubricant solution. • Wash as usual.

GENERAL WASHABLES			TRICKY ITEMS	
STAIN	SPECIAL INFORMATION	STEPS	SPECIAL INFORMATION	STEPS
Calamine Lotion (*see* Cosmetics)				
Candle Wax		• Freeze with ice and pick off gently or use edge of dull knife. • Pour boiling water through colorfast cotton and linen. • Use dry-cleaning solvent. • If necessary, repeat. • When dry, use alcohol (solvent) solution for color. • Wash. • Bleach if necessary.		• Freeze with ice and pick off gently or use edge of dull knife. • Take to the dry cleaner.
Candy, Non-Chocolate		• Apply lubricant with ¼ teaspoon of ammonia added. • If necessary, repeat. • Apply undiluted detergent. • Wash. • Use alcohol solution as solvent for color, if any. • Rinse. • Bleach as necessary.	Take to the dry cleaner if silk or wool.	• Proceed as for regular washables if not silk or wool, but use *mild* detergent.

	GENERAL WASHABLES		TRICKY ITEMS	
STAIN	SPECIAL INFORMATION	STEPS	SPECIAL INFORMATION	STEPS
Carbon Paper/ Typewriter Ribbon	Treat when fresh.	• Use dry-cleaning solvent. • Use a solution of solvent and oil if stain is stubborn. Use amyl acetate lubricant if fabric allows. • Apply dry-cleaning solvent again. • Bleach as necessary.	Treat promptly.	• Use dry-cleaning solvent. • Use a solution of cleaning solvent and a few drops of lubricant oil if stain is stubborn. • Use plain cleaning fluid. • Then use amyl acetate and again plain cleaning fluid. • Take to the dry cleaner if stain remains.
Catsup		• Apply lubricant solution. • Rinse. • Use enzyme paste. • Wash with detergent. • Bleach as necessary.	Take to the dry cleaner if silk, acetate/ triacetate, or rayon.	• Apply lubricant solution. • Rinse. • Use enzyme paste cautiously. • Wash. • Use nonchlorine bleach.
Cereals (*see* Starch)				
Chalk	Do not wet.	• Brush or lightly vacuum off. Launder.	Do not wet.	• Brush or lightly vacuum off. Launder.
Cheese		• Use dry-cleaning solvent if oily; combine with lubricant oil if stain is stubborn. • Use bar soap. • Use enzyme paste. • Bleach as necessary.	Take to the dry cleaner.	

GENERAL WASHABLES			TRICKY ITEMS	
STAIN	SPECIAL INFORMATION	STEPS	SPECIAL INFORMATION	STEPS
Chewing Gum		• Harden with ice, then pick off what you can. If any residue, use a solution of dry-cleaning solvent and oil. • Flush with plain cleaning fluid.	Take to the dry cleaner.	
Chlorine Bleach	To neutralize: Saturate with half vinegar/half water solution.	• Rinse immediately. • Neutralize. • Rinse very carefully again. • On whites, try color remover.	To neutralize: Saturate with half vinegar/half water solution. Take to the dry cleaner.	• Rinse immediately. • Neutralize. • Rinse very carefully again.
Chocolate/ Cocoa		• Rinse (with club soda if handy). • When dry, use dry-cleaning fluid. • Use bar soap. • Apply lubricant with ¼ teaspoon of ammonia added. • Wash. • Use enzyme paste. • Wash. • Bleach as necessary.	Rinse, then take to the dry cleaner.	• Rinse (with club soda if handy).

GENERAL WASHABLES			TRICKY ITEMS	
STAIN	SPECIAL INFORMATION	STEPS	SPECIAL INFORMATION	STEPS
Coffee	Take *coffee with cream* to the dry cleaner.	● Rinse. ● Apply lubricant solution with 1 teaspoon of vinegar added. ● Flush mild detergent suds with 1 tablespoon of alcohol. ● Rinse. ● Use enzyme paste. ● Wash. ● Bleach as necessary.	Take *coffee with cream* promptly to the dry cleaner.	● Rinse. ● Apply lubricant solution with 1 teaspoon of vinegar added. ● Rinse. ● Flush with 1 teaspoon of alcohol added. ● Rinse. ● Take to the dry cleaner if this doesn't work.
Condiment Sauces (soy, Worcestershire)	Take to the dry cleaner unless sturdy cotton, linen, acrylic, nylon, or polyester.	● Rinse. ● Apply lubricant solution with 1 teaspoon of vinegar added. ● Rinse. ● Use alcohol solution. ● Use enzyme paste. ● Wash.	Take to the dry cleaner.	
Cosmetics (blusher, eye shadow, face powder, lipstick, anything with zinc oxide in the ingredients)		● Use dry-cleaning solvent. ● Combine dry-cleaning solvent with lubricant oil for stubborn stains. ● Use plain cleaning fluid. ● Dry. ● Use lubricant solution with ¼ teaspoon of ammonia added. ● Rinse. ● Take to the dry cleaner if stain remains.	Take to the dry cleaner.	

GENERAL WASHABLES			TRICKY ITEMS	
STAIN	SPECIAL INFORMATION	STEPS	SPECIAL INFORMATION	STEPS
Crayon (*see* Candle Wax)	No need to freeze, but try boiling water on white or colorfast cotton or linen.		You can try dry-cleaning solvent. If that doesn't work, take to the dry cleaner.	
Cream/Milk (*see* Chocolate/Cocoa)	Rinse with plain water.		Take dried stains to the dry cleaner. Take silk to the dry cleaner.	• Use dry-cleaning fluid. • Use a combination of dry-cleaning solvent with lubricant oil. • Use plain cleaning fluid. • When dry, saturate with lubricant with a few drops of ammonia added. • Rinse well. • Use enzyme paste with caution. • Rinse. • Wash.
Depilatories/ Dentifrice	Rinse promptly. Take to the dry cleaner as soon as possible.		Rinse. Take to the dry cleaner as soon as possible.	
Deodorant	To neutralize: Saturate with a solution of 1 part vinegar to 2 parts water.	• Apply lubricant with a few drops of ammonia added. • Neutralize. • Rinse. • Use alcohol-water solution to flush color. • Rinse. • Bleach as necessary.	Take silk to the dry cleaner.	• Rinse. • Apply lubricant solution with a few drops of ammonia added. • Rinse. • Use vinegar solution. • Rinse. • Try alcohol solution if color remains.

GENERAL WASHABLES			TRICKY ITEMS	
STAIN	SPECIAL INFORMATION	STEPS	SPECIAL INFORMATION	STEPS
Dried Stains (*see* When All Else Fails . . .)	Take to the dry cleaner.			
Dye, Hair (*see* Hair Dye)				
Dyes, Fabric— Red (*see* Deodorant) **Dyes, Fabric— Non-Red**	Treat promptly.	• Rinse. • When no more color will come out, use alcohol-water solution as color solvent. • Use color remover according to package directions if fabric allows.	Treat promptly.	• Rinse. • Take to the dry cleaner.
Egg White (*see* Blood)				
Egg Yolk/Eggnog (*see* Catsup)				
Extracts (vanilla, lemon, etc.)		• Rinse. • Use lubricant solution. • Use alcohol-water solution as color solvent, if needed. • Wash.	Take silks to the dry cleaner.	• Rinse. • Apply lubricant solution. • Apply alcohol-water solution as color solvent, if needed. • Wash.
Fingernail Polish	Take to the dry cleaner unless fabric is cotton, linen, olefin, or spandex.	• Use acetone solvent if fabric tests colorfast. • Use dry-cleaning solvent when acetone has done its job.	Take to the dry cleaner.	

	GENERAL WASHABLES		TRICKY ITEMS	
STAIN	SPECIAL INFORMATION	STEPS	SPECIAL INFORMATION	STEPS
Fly Specks (insects)	If old, take to the dry cleaner.	• Rinse with warm water. • Apply lubricant solution with ¼ teaspoon of ammonia added. • Rinse and repeat if necessary. • Wash. • Bleach as necessary.	If old or on silk, take to the dry cleaner.	• Rinse in cool water. • Use lubricant solution with a few drops of ammonia added. • Rinse. • Repeat if necessary. • Wash.
Food Coloring	Treat immediately.	• Rinse. • Apply lubricant solution. • Use alcohol-water solution on remaining color. • Wash.	Treat immediately. If dried, take to the dry cleaner.	• Rinse. • Apply lubricant solution. • Use alcohol-water solution on remaining color.
Flowers		• Use enzyme paste. • Rinse. • Apply detergent, undiluted. • Wash.	Take silk to the dry cleaner.	• Use bar soap cautiously. • Rinse. • Use enzyme paste, cautiously on wool. • Wash.
Fruits and Juices	Treat promptly. Can set with age or heat.	• Rinse (let table and bed linens soak in water overnight, if you like). • Apply lubricant solution with 1 tablespoon of vinegar added. • Use enzyme paste. • Wash. • Bleach as necessary.	Treat promptly. Can set with age or heat. Take silk to dry cleaner.	• Rinse. • Apply lubricant solution with 1 teaspoon of vinegar added. • Use enzyme paste, cautiously on wool. • Wash.

GENERAL WASHABLES			TRICKY ITEMS	
STAIN	SPECIAL INFORMATION	STEPS	SPECIAL INFORMATION	STEPS
Glue, Airplane		• Use dry-cleaning solvent; combine with coconut oil on stubborn bits. • Use plain cleaning fluid. • Apply lubricant solution with 1 tablespoon of vinegar added. • Rinse. • Use enzyme paste. • Wash.	Take silk, rayon, and acetate/triacetate to cleaner.	• Use amyl acetate lubricant. • Repeat until stain is gone.
Glue, Epoxy	This stain cannot be removed.		This stain cannot be removed.	
Glue, Mucilage (*see* Glue, Airplane)			Take to the dry cleaner if on silk, or if glue is old and/or dry.	• Apply lubricant solution with a few drops of ammonia added. • Rinse. • Use enzyme paste, cautiously on wool. • Rinse.
Grape Juice (*see* Fruits and Juices)				
Grass (*see* Flowers)				
Gravy/Meat Juices		• Use bar soap. • Rinse. • Use enzyme paste. • Wash. • Bleach as necessary.	Take silk to dry cleaner.	• Use bar soap. • Rinse. • Use enzyme paste, cautiously on wool. • Wash.
Grease, Axle, etc.	Take to the dry cleaner.		Take to the dry cleaner.	

GENERAL WASHABLES			TRICKY ITEMS	
STAIN	SPECIAL INFORMATION	STEPS	SPECIAL INFORMATION	STEPS
Grease, Cooking		• Use bar soap or hard-surface cleaner. • Apply undiluted detergent suited to fabric for 1 minute. • Wash.	If old, take to the dry cleaner. Take silk to the dry cleaner.	• Use bar soap. • Rinse. • Apply lubricant solution. • Repeat if necessary.
Gum (*see* Chewing Gum)				
Hair Dye, Non-Red		• Apply lubricant solution with 1 tablespoon of vinegar added. • Rinse. • Use liquid dishwashing detergent suds with 1 tablespoon of alcohol added. • Rinse. • When dry, apply lubricant solution with ¼ teaspoon of ammonia added. • Rinse. • Wash. • Bleach as necessary.	Take to the dry cleaner promptly.	• Rinse.
Hair Dye, Red (*see* Deodorant)			Treat promptly. Take to the dry cleaner.	• Rinse.
Hair Spray (*see* Cosmetics)				• Rinse. • Use alcohol-water solution. • Rinse. • Apply lubricant solution. • Wash.

	GENERAL WASHABLES		TRICKY ITEMS	
STAIN	SPECIAL INFORMATION	STEPS	SPECIAL INFORMATION	STEPS
Hand Lotion		• Rinse with warm water. • Apply lubricant solution. • Flush well with plain water. • Wash.		• Rinse with warm water. • Apply lubricant solution. • Flush well with plain water. • Wash.
Hemline Stains	If old, take to the dry cleaner.	• Presoak in lukewarm water. • Use bar soap or hard-surface cleaner. • Rinse. • Repeat if necessary. • Wash, working on each area of stain by hand. • If stain remains, take to the dry cleaner.	Take old or stubborn stains to the dry cleaner.	• Use bar soap cautiously. • Rinse. • Repeat if necessary. • Wash, working on each area of stain by hand.
Honey (*see* Sugar/Syrup)				
Ice Cream, Chocolate (*see* Chocolate/Cocoa)				
Ice Cream, Non-Chocolate		• Rinse with warm water and use bar soap. • Use enzyme paste. • Bleach as necessary.	Take silk to the dry cleaner.	• Rinse with lukewarm water and use bar soap gently. • Use enzyme paste, cautiously on wool. Use nonchlorine bleach.

GENERAL WASHABLES			TRICKY ITEMS	
STAIN	SPECIAL INFORMATION	STEPS	SPECIAL INFORMATION	STEPS
Ink, Ballpoint (*see* When All Else Fails . . .)		• Rinse. • Apply lubricant solution with ¼ teaspoon of ammonia added. • Flush with half vinegar/half water solution. • Use alcohol-water solution. • Bleach or use color remover as necessary if fabric allows.	Treat fresh or take to the dry cleaner.	• Rinse. • Apply lubricant solution with a few drops of ammonia added. • Use half vinegar/half water solution. • Repeat. • Take to the dry cleaner if stain remains.
Ink, Felt-Tip	Try method here, then try method for Cosmetics if necessary.	• Rinse with warm water, being careful to contain stain by using a small amount. • Use alcohol-water solution. • Apply lubricant solution with ¼ teaspoon of ammonia added. • Wash.	Treat fresh or take to the dry cleaner.	• Rinse with warm water, being careful to contain stain by using a small amount. • Use alcohol-water solution on color. • Take to the dry cleaner if stain remains.
Ink, India (*see* Cosmetics)	If doesn't respond to Cosmetics method, try steps given here.	• Apply enzyme paste. • Take to the dry cleaner.	Take to the dry cleaner.	
Ink, Mimeograph (*see* Carbon Paper/ Typewriter Ribbon)	Treat promptly.			

	GENERAL WASHABLES		TRICKY ITEMS	
STAIN	SPECIAL INFORMATION	STEPS	SPECIAL INFORMATION	STEPS
Ink, Red		• Use alcohol-water solution. • Apply lubricant solution with ¼ teaspoon of ammonia added. • Use half vinegar/half water solution to flush. • Repeat if necessary. • Bleach or use color remover as necessary.		• Use alcohol-water solution. • Apply lubricant solution, with a few drops ammonia added. • Flush with solution of 1 part vinegar with 1 part water. • Wash.
Insecticides		• Use bar soap. • Try dry-cleaning solvent and oil. • Use plain cleaning fluid.	Take to the dry cleaner.	
Iodine	Rinse *immediately* or it will dye fabric. Take to the dry cleaner.	• Rinse with warm water. Can be removed with color remover from whites only.	Rinse immediately or it will dye fabric. Take to the dry cleaner.	• Rinse with warm water.
Jam/Jelly (*see* Beets and Berries *or* Fruits and Juices *depending on type*)				
Lemon Juice (*see* Acids)				
Lipstick (*see* Cosmetics)			Take to the dry cleaner.	
Liqueurs (*see* Alcoholic Beverages)				

	GENERAL WASHABLES		TRICKY ITEMS	
STAIN	SPECIAL INFORMATION	STEPS	SPECIAL INFORMATION	STEPS
Lotion, Suntan		• Use hard-surface household cleaner. • Use enzyme paste. • Rinse after 15 minutes. Repeat if necessary. • Wash with detergent.	Take silk to the dry cleaner.	• Use enzyme paste, cautiously on wool. • Rinse after a minute or two and repeat if method is working. • Wash.
Mayonnaise (*see* Gravy/Meat Juices)	Take old stains to the dry cleaner.		Take old stains to the dry cleaner.	
Mercurochrome/ Merthiolate		• Rinse. • Apply lubricant with ¼ teaspoon of ammonia added. • Try half vinegar/half water solution. • Rinse. • Use alcohol-water solution. • Rinse. • Bleach or use color remover as necessary.	Take to dry cleaner if home method doesn't work.	• Rinse. • Apply lubricant solution with 1 teaspoon of alcohol added. • Rinse. • Repeat if working.
Metal Polish		• Rinse. • Use bar soap. • Rinse well. • If color changes, apply a few drops of ammonia. • Rinse after 1 minute.	Take silk and wool to the dry cleaner after rinse step.	• Rinse. • Use bar soap. • Rinse well. • If color changes, apply a few drops of ammonia. • Rinse after 1 minute.
Metal Tarnish	Take to the dry cleaner.		Take to the dry cleaner.	
Mildew (*see* When All Else Fails . . .)				

	GENERAL WASHABLES		TRICKY ITEMS	
STAIN	SPECIAL INFORMATION	STEPS	SPECIAL INFORMATION	STEPS
Milk (*see* Chocolate/ Cocoa)			Take silk to the dry cleaner after rinsing.	• Rinse. • Use enzyme paste, cautiously on wool. • Rinse. • Repeat if necessary until stain is gone.
Mimeograph Correction Fluid (*see* Carbon Paper/ Typewriter Ribbon)				
Molasses (*see* Candy)			Take silk to the dry cleaner after rinsing.	• Rinse. • Wash.
Mud	See comment under scraping information, p. 19. If sticky, take to the dry cleaner.	• Use bar soap after surface particles have been removed. • Wash.	Take to the dry cleaner if spot remains after rinsing.	• Rinse. • Wash.
Mustard	Take to the dry cleaner if old or on good clothes. A very difficult stain to remove.	• Rinse. • Use bar soap. • Use alcohol solution. • Wash if stain basically gone; if not, take to the dry cleaner.	Take to the dry cleaner, unless on spandex. A very difficult stain to remove.	• Rinse. • Use bar soap. • Use alcohol-water (solvent) solution. • Wash. • Repeat if necessary.
Nicotine (*see* Tobacco)				
Oil, Bath		• Use lubricant with ¼ teaspoon of ammonia added. • Repeat if necessary. • Rinse. • Use enzyme paste. • Wash.		• Apply lubricant with a few drops of ammonia added. • Repeat if necessary. • Use enzyme paste, cautiously on wool. • Wash.
Oil, Salad (*see* Grease Cooking)				

GENERAL WASHABLES			TRICKY ITEMS	
STAIN	SPECIAL INFORMATION	STEPS	SPECIAL INFORMATION	STEPS
Paint, Latex	ALERT! Treat before it dries.	• Rinse with warm water. • Use alcohol-water solution. • Rinse again. • Wash.	ALERT! Rinse before it dries. Take to the dry cleaner if home method isn't working.	• Rinse in lukewarm water. • Use alcohol-water (solvent) solution on color. • Rinse again. • Wash.
Paint, Oil-Base	Take promptly to the dry cleaner. These vary in content.		Take promptly to the dry cleaner.	
Paint, Watercolor (*see* Ink, Felt-Tip, *except see* Mustard *for yellow paint,* Deodorant *for red*)		• If any residual color, bleach as necessary or use color remover if the fabric allows.	These vary in content. If home method isn't working, take to the dry cleaner.	• Rinse. • Use alcohol-water (solvent) solution on residual color. • Wash.
Peanut Butter		• Use bar soap. • Rinse. • When dry, use a solution of cleaning solvent and oil on stubborn stains. • Flush with plain cleaning fluid.	Rinse silk, wash with mild detergent. Take to the dry cleaner if stain remains.	• Rinse. • Use bar soap. • When dry, use a solution of dry-cleaning solvent and oil on stubborn stains. • Use plain cleaning fluid.
Pencil (*see* When All Else Fails . . .)				
Perfume	Rinse promptly.	• Rinse. • Apply lubricant. • Rinse. • Use alcohol-water solution as solvent. • Rinse.	Rinse silk. Apply lubricant solution. Take to the dry cleaner if stain remains.	• Rinse. • Apply lubricant solution. • Rinse. • Use alcohol-water solution on remaining color. • Rinse. • Wash.

GENERAL WASHABLES			TRICKY ITEMS	
STAIN	SPECIAL INFORMATION	STEPS	SPECIAL INFORMATION	STEPS
Perspiration (*see* When All Else Fails . . .)			Treat promptly: rings may be permanent.	• Rinse with warm water. • Use mild detergent. • Rinse. • Apply lubricant solution with a few drops ammonia added if heavy staining. Rinse well. • Use alcohol-water (solvent) solution on rings. • Rinse.
Pet Droppings	Scrape up as much as possible.	• Rinse with warm water or club soda. • Apply lubricant with ¼ teaspoon of ammonia added. • Rinse. • Repeat if necessary. • Use enzyme paste. • Soak in water to which a tablespoon of baking soda has been added. • Wash.	Scrape up as much as possible. Take silk to the dry cleaner.	• Rinse with warm water or club soda. • Apply lubricant with a few drops of ammonia added. • Rinse. • Use enzyme paste, cautiously on wool. • Soak 10 minutes in water to which 1 tablespoon of baking soda has been added. • Wash.
Putty	Take to the dry cleaner.		Take to the dry cleaner.	
Road Splashes (*see* Mud)	If more than just mud, take to the dry cleaner.		If more than just mud, take to the dry cleaner.	

	GENERAL WASHABLES		TRICKY ITEMS	
STAIN	SPECIAL INFORMATION	STEPS	SPECIAL INFORMATION	STEPS
Rubber Cement	Rub up or pick off as much as you can.	• Use dry-cleaning solvent. • Use a cleaning solution of solvent and lubricant oil on stubborn stains. • Flush with plain cleaning fluid.	Rub up as much as you can, or pick off gently.	• Use dry-cleaning solvent, then a solution of cleaning solvent and oil. Use plain cleaning fluid.
Rust	Take to the dry cleaner. See also lemon juice/salt "bleaching" on page 49.		Take to the dry cleaner.	
Salad Dressing	Treat promptly. If you cannot use the regular method promptly, apply absorbent powder. Take to the dry cleaner if method fails.	• Use bar soap, then hard-surface cleaner prior to washing. • Use enzyme paste. • Wash again.	Take to the dry cleaner if home method isn't working or if silk.	• Use absorbent powder, if treatment must wait. • Use bar soap cautiously. • Rinse and wash. • When dry, use dry-cleaning solvent.
Sauces, Barbecue/ Spaghetti		• Use bar soap. • Rinse. • Apply lubricant with ¼ teaspoon of ammonia added. Repeat if necessary. • Use enzyme paste. • Soak in warm water for an hour. • Wash. • Bleach as necessary.	Take dried stains, silk, and wool to the dry cleaner.	• Rinse. • Use bar soap cautiously. • Rinse. • Apply lubricant with a few drops ammonia added. • Use enzyme paste. • Soak 15 minutes in lukewarm water. • Wash.

	GENERAL WASHABLES		TRICKY ITEMS	
STAIN	SPECIAL INFORMATION	STEPS	SPECIAL INFORMATION	STEPS
Scorch	Many are on fabric surface and can be removed.	● Rinse. ● Apply undiluted detergent to the spot for 5 minutes. ● Wash. ● Bleach as necessary.	Many are on fabric surface and can be removed.	● Rinse. ● Apply mild detergent, undiluted, to the spot for 5 minutes. ● Wash. ● Use nonchlorine bleach as necessary.
Shellac	Take to the dry cleaner if home method isn't working.	● Use dry-cleaning solvent, then a combination of cleaning solvent and lubricant oil. ● Flush with plain cleaning fluid. ● Dry. ● Use alcohol-water solution. ● Rinse.	Take to the dry cleaner promptly.	
Shoe Polish, Black (*see* Cosmetics)			Take to the dry cleaner.	
Shoe Polish, Brown (*see* Hair Dye)			Take to the dry cleaner.	
Shoe Polish, White (*see* Shellac)	End by flushing with amyl acetate. Rinse.		Take to the dry cleaner.	
Shoe Polish, Non-White (*see* Cosmetics)			Take to the dry cleaner.	
Smoke/Soot	Take to the dry cleaner.			

GENERAL WASHABLES			TRICKY ITEMS	
STAIN	SPECIAL INFORMATION	STEPS	SPECIAL INFORMATION	STEPS
Soft Drinks		● Rinse. ● Use lubricant solution. ● Use alcohol-water solution on color traces. ● Use enzyme paste. ● Wash. ● Bleach as necessary.	Take to the dry cleaner if home method isn't working.	● Rinse. ● Apply lubricant solution. ● Use alcohol-water (solvent) solution for remaining color. ● Wash.
Solder	Take to the dry cleaner.		Take to the dry cleaner.	
Soup, Cream (*see* Chocolate/ Cocoa)	Skip step involving club soda.			
Soup, Meat-Base (*see* Blood)				
Soup, Vegetable		● Rinse. ● Apply lubricant with ¼ teaspoon of ammonia added. ● Rinse. ● Use bar soap. ● Wash. ● Use alcohol-water solution for color.	Take silk to the dry cleaner.	● Rinse. ● Apply lubricant with a few drops ammonia added. ● Rinse. ● Use bar soap cautiously on wool. ● Wash. ● Use alcohol-water (solvent) solution on remaining color. ● Rinse.
Starch, (flour/bread, etc.)	Dries stiff. Dry patch turns white when scratched. Never apply heat if starch content possible!	● Rinse. ● Use enzyme paste if stain remains after working water through it.	Take silk to the dry cleaner.	● Rinse. ● Use enzyme paste, cautiously on wool. ● Wash.

	GENERAL WASHABLES		TRICKY ITEMS	
STAIN	SPECIAL INFORMATION	STEPS	SPECIAL INFORMATION	STEPS
Sugar/Syrup	Dries stiff. Dry patch turns white when scratched.	● Rinse with warm water. ● Wash.		● Rinse. ● Wash.
Tea (*see* Coffee)				
Tobacco	Never use heat if tobacco suspected!	● Rinse. ● Apply lubricant with 1 tablespoon of vinegar added. ● Rinse. ● Use alcohol-water solution to remove color. ● Use enzyme paste. ● Wash. ● Bleach as necessary.	Never use heat if tobacco stain suspected. Take to the dry cleaner.	
Tomato (*see* Beets and Berries)				
Typewriter Correction Fluid (Wite-Out, Liquid Paper, etc.)	Water-base (stated on the bottle) types wash out; oil-base or paint types *don't* and are likely to be permanent. Don't try paint thinner.	Water-base: ● Rinse. ● Wash remainder out with mild soap suds. Oil-base: ● *Do not rinse.* Blot up as much as possible. ● Take to the dry cleaner *quickly.*		Water-base: ● Rinse spot and wash when fabric will stand it. Otherwise, take to the dry cleaner. Oil-base: ● Take to the dry cleaner quickly.

GENERAL WASHABLES			TRICKY ITEMS	
STAIN	SPECIAL INFORMATION	STEPS	SPECIAL INFORMATION	STEPS
Urine	Treat before it dries.	• Rinse (with club soda if handy). • Apply lubricant with 1 tablespoon of vinegar added. • Apply lubricant with ¼ teaspoon of ammonia added. • Rinse. • Use alcohol solution as solvent for color. • Rinse. • Bleach as necessary.	Take old stains to the dry cleaner. Treat before it dries if possible.	• Rinse. • Use vinegar-water solution, then lubricant with a few drops of ammonia added. • Rinse. • Use nonchlorine bleach as necessary.
Varnish	Take to the dry cleaner.		Take to the dry cleaner.	
Vegetables (*see* Soup)				
Vinegar, Colored	Treat as Acid. Then follow method for Alcoholic Beverages.		Treat as Acid. Then follow method for Alcoholic Beverages.	
Water Spots	Some fabrics water-spot permanently. See the fabric guide (Chapter 12) for which ones do.	• Wash entire item. If spot doesn't disappear, treat as an unknown stain. (p. 50).	Some fabrics water-spot permanently. See the fabric guide (Chapter 12) for which ones do.	• Wash entire item. If spot doesn't disappear, treat as an unknown stain (p. 50), but use only gentle stain removers.

	GENERAL WASHABLES		TRICKY ITEMS	
STAIN	SPECIAL INFORMATION	STEPS	SPECIAL INFORMATION	STEPS
Wax, Auto/Floor/ Furniture	Take good clothes to the dry cleaner.	• Use dry-cleaning solvent, then a solution of cleaning solvent and lubricant oil on stubborn stains. • Use plain cleaning fluid. • When dry, apply lubricant with ¼ teaspoon of ammonia added. • Wash. • Bleach as necessary.	Take silk to the dry cleaner.	• Use dry-cleaning solvent, then a solution of cleaning solvent and oil on stubborn stains, then plain cleaning fluid. • When dry, apply lubricant with a few drops of ammonia added. • Wash.
Wax Remover	Take to the dry cleaner.		Take to the dry cleaner.	
Wine, White/Red (*see* Alcoholic Beverages)				
Yellow Stains	Take to the dry cleaner if old.	• Rinse. • Use bar soap. • Use alcohol-water solution. • Wash.	Take to the dry cleaner if old.	• Rinse. • Use bar soap. • Use alcohol-water (solvent) solution. • Wash.

WHEN ALL ELSE FAILS . . .

Ink: If the method on the chart doesn't work, let the material dry, after rinsing, and soak in a solution of enzyme presoak and water. Tamp or work gently after 5 minutes. Rinse. If a little stain remains, soak the area in the detergent/glycerin cleaner given on p. 18 with a few drops of ammonia added. Then rinse well. Finish by bleaching if the fabric will take it.

- If the ink is *water-soluble* (it may say so on the pen), use soap or detergent to presoak, then wash. Bleach if necessary.
- On cotton or linen or synthetic upholstery, try hair spray or dry-cleaning fluid if the stain is fresh. Then

flush with small amounts of the detergent/glycerin cleaner with water. Next, rinse carefully with plain water. Unless the material is wool, you can dry with a hairdryer on low heat and at low speed.

Mildew: Preventing the growth of this fungus is no problem if the clothes are put away dry and the storage area is kept dry and cool. But before storing linens for a long period, rinse them in water to which a teaspoon or so of lemon juice has been added. Be sure they are dry before putting them away.

If you find mildew, see the closet cleanup method in Chapter 6, and try one of the following methods on the clothes:

- Presoak washable cotton, linen, and ramie in the hottest water and strongest detergent possible and then use a mild bleach solution. If this doesn't work and the material is white, try color remover as directed on the package. Use elbow grease on sturdy fabrics.
- Old mildew stains on whites can sometimes be "bleached" with a paste of salt and lemon juice.
- With sturdy white cotton and linen items, you can also try boiling them in plenty of soap and water with 2 or 3 tablespoons of chlorine or all-fabric bleach added.
- Washable rayon, silk, and wool can be treated with potassium permanganate (a drugstore item) *if* they are colorfast, but this is an emergency measure. Make a solution with enough water to cover and 1 tablespoon of potassium permanganate. Let soak for a minute or two, then rinse carefully. Commercial mildew removers are not for clothes.
- Canvas shoes, bags, and so forth can be cleaned with a paste of scouring powder and water, rubbed in gently. Let sit a few minutes and check progress. Reapply if necessary, then rinse well. CAUTION: The bleach in scouring powder will often lighten colors. To give an even tone, apply the paste over the whole item.

Pencil: Graphite pencil may respond to dry-cleaning fluid. Tamp. Let dry. Then proceed with a detergent/glycerin application as for ink. Rinse well. Take to the dry cleaner if this method doesn't work.

Perspiration: Dry cleaning won't remove perspiration, but washing will. (The acid and organic contents of sweat affect dyes, making silk and all "Dry Clean Only" clothes a bad bet in hot weather.)

- For washables: launder clothes more often in summer or when you're active. Perspiration can damage fabric even when there's no visible stain. Use the normal water temperature for the clothes and add 1 teaspoon of borax or baking soda per 2 gallons water and 1 teaspoon of ammonia if the clothes are cotton or linen.
- If you need to flush perspiration out of silk or rayon, squeeze a little water to which a *few drops* of ammonia have been added through the affected area. Then flush with plain water thoroughly, let dry, and take clothes to the dry cleaner.

Sticky Stains: Most such stains are sugar-based, and if the fabric is washable can be rinsed out with cool or lukewarm water. Sticky substances attract dirt, and since the stains are more difficult to get out the longer they're left in, try to get to them promptly.

Unknown Stains: On washable clothes: If *fresh*, do the usual emergency steps and then decide whether the stain is greasy, nongreasy (i.e., water-soluble), or complex. Use grease solvents suited to the fabric on greasy or complex stains, then an appropriate detergent and lukewarm water. Saturate *non*greasy stains with handwashing liquid with a few drops of glycerin added, then wash out. Follow with laundry bar soap if the stain is resistant.

Plagued by spot-cleaning rings? If dry-cleaning fluid was used, try steaming with either a teakettle at a brisk boil or the extra-steam unit in your iron. Move the stream of steam in a circular path from the center of the spot out beyond the ring, being careful that the material does not get wet, causing more spots. Very good for many silks and wools.

If the stain is *old* and stiff, submerge it in a saucer of water in which ¼ teaspoon of baking soda has been dissolved. After 10 minutes, rinse with plain water, then flush with 2 tablespoons of water stirred up with a few drops of ammonia. Continue as for nongreasy stains. If the spot is *old* and *not* stiff, saturate the stain with grease solvent suited to the fabric, then wash after 5 or 10 minutes. (Repeat if necessary to get the last of the stain out.) With machine-washables and synthetics, saturate remaining stain with undiluted laundry detergent for a few minutes, then wash it out. For wool, silk, rayon, acetate, or triacetate, rub in laundry bar soap, wash it out, then handwash the clothes as usual.

With the right equipment and a methodical approach, you can remove just about any damned spot.

And when you can't, the dry cleaner often can.

CHAPTER THREE

Loads on Laundry

Have you ever asked yourself why your stack of newly clean laundry doesn't resemble the bright, fluffy, perfectly clean specimens on TV? If so, you need this chapter, in which the laundering process is broken down into steps. With this clear plan it is much easier to see what changes might be needed to give more satisfactory results.

Basically, the process goes like this: Soap or detergent and water penetrate the cloth fibers, make a bond with dirt molecules, and then float them away in the rinsing process. What you can do is influence the parts of the laundering process over which you have control: softening hard water so that it will make plenty of suds, for example, or using less soap or detergent if your area has soft water so that the wash isn't gummy. In a hurry? You might decide to wash in hot water because it penetrates much more quickly than cold.

Since there are now man-made fibers as well as the familiar natural ones (cotton, linen, ramie, silk, and wool), you should learn how these behave and launder them according to their needs. The Fiber Treatment Chart tells you what these needs are.

When you buy something new and different, wash it separately the first time, following the care label but also using the Fiber Treatment Chart. If you are in doubt about something, you can also refer to the fiber and fabric guides (Chapter 12). The more you know about what you wash, the better your laundry-room decisions will be.

MACHINE-LAUNDERING FUNDAMENTALS —————————

A well-equipped laundry shelf sets the stage for fresh, clean, attractive clothes. You can do a really good job with the following basics plus as many of the optional items as you find a use for.

WHAT YOU NEED —————————

Water Softeners

- Borax (safe with all fabrics/fibers and cleaning agents), for use in medium-hard to hard water. It also deodorizes.
  Optional: washing soda (but it can precipitate minerals, leaving flecks on clothes).

Prespotters and Presoaks

- a *laundry* bar soap such as Fels-Naptha, Kirkman, or Octagon, for "ring around the collar" problems. Sometimes call "borax soap."
- a liquid household cleaner such as Lestoil, labeled for use on clothes, for grease spots (also known as a hard-surface cleaner, since it is usually used on tile, formica, etc.).
- automatic dishwasher detergent in powder form, for getting stubborn stains and graying or yellowing out of polyester, nylon, acrylic, modacrylic, and synthetic/cotton blends (*not for use in the washing machine*).
  Optional: • an enzyme laundry booster (presoak), for protein-containing spots. • spray, stick, or liquid prespotter, for grease stains. • baking soda, to revive faded cotton, linen, and washable wool and as a deodorant.

Soap and Detergent

- regular granular laundry detergent, *without* added bleach, for washing sturdy fibers.
- plain soap flakes or powder, or white or clear dishwashing liquid, for fabrics that can't take regular laun-

---

*Soap is perfectly fine for all washing *if* the wash water is soft or has been softened. But synthetic detergents (soap cleans, so it is actually a detergent, too) may give better results on heavy greasy dirt, in hard water, and with man-made fibers that attract greasy dirt. Detergents also have controlled or low suds, which means they won't clog the machine.

dry detergents, which are harsh cleaning agents. Use for handwashing and for gentle machine washing wherever the water is soft to medium-soft.*

Optional: concentrated, heavy-duty liquid detergent, for presoaking and washing very dirty sturdy fabrics.

Bleach and Other Additives

- chlorine bleach, for whitening or brightening white and colorfast fabrics (safe on fibers as listed on the Fiber Treatment Chart) and for disinfecting.
- plain distilled vinegar, for neutralizing after chlorine bleaching or bleach or ammonia spills and for reviving color in old cotton and linen.
- plain household ammonia, for adding to regular laundry to cut greasy grime (an alkaline cleaner, so safe only on fibers as listed on the Fiber Treatment Chart under "Alkaline Cleaners").

Optional: • All fabric bleach. • Fabric softener. • Bluing.

Equipment

- a clothes brush, for getting rid of surface dust.
- a ½-inch-wide, long-handled paintbrush, for applying liquid prespotters. An old toothbrush is perfect.
- an unbreakable measuring cup, to control the amount of cleaning agent added.
- a gallon plastic jug, for measuring water. (An extra one can be used to carry your premixed washing agents to the laundromat.)
- 1 or preferably 2 wicker hampers,* to ensure that air can circulate around dirty laundry, preventing mold and odors. NOTE: To clean, sponge with a solution of 1 teaspoon of salt, 2 tablespoons of baking soda and 1 cup of water.
- plenty of old towels, for spot removal, mopping up, cleaning the hampers and the washing machine drum, etc.
- 1 or 2 nylon-mesh zippered bags, to protect delicate fabrics in the wash.

Optional: • clothesline or rack. • clothespins and a washable bag for them that can be clipped or hung from the line.

*Two hampers are a good safety measure. The first is to hold general washables, the second to keep both hand washables and new clothes, which need special attention, from getting mixed in with regular laundry.

SIX STEPS TO CLEANER CLOTHES ————————————————

1. *Check It Out*

Before you even begin laundering, consider the following:

- *Is your water hard, medium hard, or soft?* To find out, consult a water-conditioning or agricultural extension service, or a local home economics department. About two thirds of the United States has hard to very hard water. Soften water as needed, either by having your water system conditioned or as described below, p. 57.
- *Are the clothes you are going to machine-wash sturdily constructed?* Also, are the dyes fast enough and the finish permanent enough to hold up under machine-washing conditions? Mend or at least pin any rips or tears before laundering.
- *Are you observing care labels?* Follow label directions, and whenever possible, lean toward the milder cleaning agents and gentler cleaning methods: warm, not hot, water; presoaking rather than chlorine bleaching; a lower drying temperature or line drying. Keep in mind that care labels will tell you a safe method but not the *only* method. In fact, each instruction allows for the use of any agent or method easier on clothes than the one given. For example, "Machine Wash" allows for handwashing or dry cleaning, "Warm Water Wash" for washing in either cold or warm water. But the word "only" used in regard to washing *does* mean not to do anything else.

2. *Sorting*

Why sort? Because it keeps dyes and soil from darker or dirtier clothes away from light fabrics—particularly nylon, which usually picks up color easily (and permanently). You also get a chance to catch and pretreat stains so they don't set, tie up strings and ribbons so they don't pull out or knot, button buttons so clothes keep their shape, zip zippers so they don't snag other clothes, and clean out pockets. If the washing machine's drum is chipped, this is the time to protect sheer and other easily snagged fabrics by putting them in a mesh bag.

Remove any items that must be handwashed or

Is "ring around the collar" just an advertising fabrication? No. But the best way to deal with it is *prevention*. Before getting dressed, swab around your neck, waist, and wrists with a mild astringent like witch hazel. Repeat after vigorous exercise. Urge all family members to do the same.

washed separately, and turn items made from fabrics that produce lint—knits, cotton towels, flannel, and other fuzzies, acrylic/modacrylic, and brushed polyester—inside out if you don't do them separately. The rule is: *When in doubt, turn inside out.*

PROCEDURE FOR SORTING

- Much of the time you can get away with sorting into two loads: light colors and dark or strong colors. A third load would be delicate articles that need the Gentle/Knit/Delicate cycle with its slow agitation and spin. These come out best if the load is small. (Red, purple, and dark blue are the colors that run the longest, so they must be washed separately or with like colors until you are sure they no longer release color.) Noncolorfast fabrics *must* be washed separately.
- If you want, sort out the very dirty light-colored clothes for presoaking or for a separate hot-water wash, using the appropriate additives to get out tough dirt. You may want to use ammonia or bleach with this load, for example.
- If it isn't too much trouble, make up a load of very dirty dark clothes in heavyweight fabrics like denim. These sturdy workweight fabrics may need presoaking. See the section on washing for the appropriate method of cleaning.

NOTE: The cost of dryer drying is high, but laundering costs pennies. Don't worry about the expense of multiple laundry loads.

All the whites gone pink because Bobby put his red wool turtleneck in the washer when no one was looking? Buy a package or two of color remover (in the dye rack at the five-and-ten) and use the stove-top method given on the package to get cotton, polycotton, nylon, or durable press white again. Color remover is also great for removing rust, some inks, and iodine.

3. Prespotting and Presoaking

Pre*spotting* attacks specific stains, while pre*soaking* copes with general ingrained grease and grime, either by extended submersion in a soap or detergent solution or by a brief immersion in a stronger cleaning solution specifically suited to the problem being attacked.

Pretreating of any kind, while not always necessary, often helps you avoid harsher methods of cleaning such as heavy chlorine bleaching and scrubbing; it also cuts down on the necessity to add bluing or brighteners. *Always* launder after presoaking, since soaking loosens dirt but does not wholly remove it.

Refer to the stain chart in Chapter 2 to deal with a specific stain, but here is a summary of standard prespotting and presoaking methods:

GREASY/OILY SPOTS ON COLORFAST FABRICS

- When the Fiber Treatment Chart indicates the fiber is tough, paint or dribble on a few drops of hard-surface liquid cleaner. Leave for about 5 minutes. To be sure you remove the spot, use a small brush like a toothbrush to rub the spot, and then wash and rinse by hand. Wash the whole item as usual.
- For *all* fibers and fabrics except silk, rub in lather from a laundry bar soap. You can use some elbow grease on sturdy weaves and knits. This is the most generally useful way to attack all kinds of grimy spots, including the dirt embedded in kids' jackets.
- *Spray prespotters* are often helpful, but since the clothes go straight into the wash, you won't know until after laundering if the spot is gone; by then it may have set. Do not use spray prespotters on wool, acetate, triacetate, silk, or spandex.

CAUTION: Don't let any of the above cleaning substances dry on the clothes. Rinse out well. Do not use in conjunction with a wash containing bleach or bluing.

DINGY COTTONS

- As long as the cotton is sturdy, try this: make up a sinkful of the hottest suds the fabric will stand, using regular or heavy-duty detergent. Add ¼ cup of borax if water needs softening. Squeeze suds through gently for a few minutes, rubbing with a soft brush where necessary to dislodge dirt. Leave for 30 minutes to 1 hour or until suds begin to subside. Rinse, then wash as usual. If this doesn't work, try presoaking in a mild chlorine bleach solution: about 1 tablespoon per gallon of water. Stir in well. Add wet clothes. Leave for an hour or more, stirring often. NOTE: *Clothes must be colorfast.*
- If the cotton isn't sturdy, use cool water, liquid dishwasher detergent, or soap with 1 tablespoon of baking soda per gallon of water. Stir to dissolve, and soak for 15 to 30 minutes. Avoid rubbing or rub very gently. Rinse and drain without lifting the clothes out of the sink, as the weight of the water can drag wet yarns out of shape. If this is only partially effective, repeat. Wash as usual.

DINGY SYNTHETICS AND BLENDS

- Simply dissolve about 3 tablespoons of powdered automatic dishwasher detergent in a couple of gallons of

warm water. Add one or two items and squeeze the solution through them, rubbing bad spots. Remove after
3 or 4 minutes and rinse very well. Wash if necessary.
• Use this mixture only on polyester, nylon, acrylic,
modacrylic, and synthetic/cotton blends. This very alkaline cleaner must be used with care . . . and rubber
gloves. Use only occasionally. It is great for uniforms
and sports outfits like hockey jerseys.

PROTEIN-BASED PROBLEMS
• If the stains are extensive, it may be easiest to presoak
for an hour or two using an enzyme laundry booster.
Do not use on silk or wools or other alkaline-sensitive
fibers. (See "Alkaline Cleaners" on the Fiber Treatment
Chart if you're not sure which these are.)

**GREASY, GRIMY LOADS, ESPECIALLY COTTON
AND COTTON/POLYESTER BLENDS**
• Add ¼ cup of ammonia to the sudsy water.

4. Washing
• *Don't overstuff the washer.* About three fourths full is
right. Overcrowding wrinkles fabrics, (especially man-
mades and permanent press) and may stop the machine by throwing it off balance or even breaking it.
Small items can get between the inner drum and outer
casing, jamming the mechanism. Use plenty of water.
• If your owner's manual gives a maximum *weight*—say,
6½ pounds of dry clothes—put in less than that when
you're working with synthetics and permanent press.
The standard weight is for cotton, which is heavier per
square inch, so it takes up less space than synthetics.
• *Add soap or detergent.* Regular detergent with few or
no additives works best for regular laundry—no need
to blitz the laundry with a product containing a little
of everything. About ½ to ¾ cup of regular powdered
detergent or ⅓ cup of soap powder is enough for
the average load. Other measurements: either ¼ cup
of liquid concentrated detergent or ¾ to 1 cup of regular powdered detergent for a heavier, dirtier load in
hard water.
• If bleach or fabric softener is necessary, fill the dis-
pensers. *Do not add directly to the wash.*
• In picking the wash and rinse cycle, suit the water
temperature, level of agitation, and spin speed to the

Bank on borax: Add
about ¼ cup per regular
machine load. It loosens
soil, sweetens sour
smells, and softens
water (and two thirds of
America has hard water).
Keeps the diaper pail
fresh-smelling, too.

clothes that predominate in the load, as below. However, the Permanent Press cycle works well for all normal-size, mixed fabric, normally dirty loads.

WASH RINSE GUIDE

TEMPERATURE	SPIN	PURPOSE
Hot/Warm or Hot/Cold	Normal agitation and normal spin	To get very heavy fabrics, very dirty cottons, linen, or polycotton really clean.
Warm/Cold (also called Regular) and Permanent Press	Normal agitation and normal or slow spin	For standard mixed loads of permanent press, cotton, linen, polyester, polycotton, acrylic, nylon, and blends. NOTE: The cold rinse reduces wrinkling of man-mades and permanent press items.
Cold/Cold	Slow agitation and slow spin (may be called Gentle, Delicate or Knit cycle)	Cold-water wash items, acetate, triacetate, olefin, rayon, spandex blends, wool if machine-washable, small, lightly soiled loads of lightweight cotton, linen, polyester, or nylon. NOTE: Spandex can be washed according to the predominant fiber in the blend, but choose cooler temperatures and hang to dry.

TIME SETTINGS FOR THE WASH

2 to 3 minutes for Delicate/Knit cycle, small loads, lightly soiled clothes.

5 to 7 minutes for standard mixed loads of moderately dirty clothes.

10 minutes or more for loads with heavy or very dirty materials and large loads (also if bleach is used).

SUGGESTIONS

- Using cold water to wash does save energy, but cold water isn't as effective as warm or hot water. With cold water, use more detergent than usual, extend the wash time, use a little extra water softener, and keep the load small to medium in size.

- Be sure to *rinse well.* Dirt bonds to the soap or detergent molecule; as long as any suds residue remains,
clothes won't look or be clean. Clothes that smell very
soapy or feel at all gummy or slippery should be run
through an extra rinse. Thorough rinsing is especially
important after you have used bluing or a fabric softener and when fabrics have a flame-retardant finish.

5. Drying

MACHINE DRYING

It's vital to sort for the dryer as well as for the washer.
For example, some clothes must be hung to dry—see
"Line Drying". (Line drying not only saves money—heat
for the dryer is the major energy cost of laundering—but
reduces wear and tear on the clothes.) Also, lightweight
man-made fiber clothes, which dry out in 5 to 15 minutes, typically wrinkle badly and collect static unless
dried only briefly on a low setting. Clothes that have to
be ironed *needn't* be machine dried.

- After setting aside clothes that don't need machine
(tumble) drying, decide whether to consolidate clothes
from several washloads into one grand dryer load or to
separate into two stacks. Of course be sure that
clothes have room to tumble freely to forestall wrinkling and wear from abrasion.
- If you do one *mixed* load, use the Permanent Press or
low setting, since this gives the best results with all
kinds of fabric. Check after 15 minutes or so and remove any dry clothes. This is the best way to prevent
static buildup, lint pickup, and wrinkling. *Don't let
clothes get bone dry.* A touch of moisture benefits all
fibers.
- If you do *separate* loads, one should be quick-drying
fabrics such as nylon, acrylic/modacrylic, polyester,
permanent press, lightweight polycottons, spandex,
and olefin. Do these on a Permanent Press or low setting, since it has a cooldown at the end of the cycle
that minimizes wrinkling. Remove clothes as they dry.
(If the dryer has only Heat and No Heat/Air Dry, get
mostly dry on Heat, then run 5 minutes or so on No
Heat/Air Dry. Extend times as necessary.) The second
load will be the longer-drying items such as cottons,
linens, and heavyweight polycotton. Do on the regular
or Permanent Press setting.

**When sneakers need
washing, put them in the
machine with a couple
of towels to minimize
banging and wear. Use
warm, not hot, water.
Dry in fresh air or buy
the rack that comes with
some dryers made
especially for drying
things like sneakers.
Remove before
completely dry. To get
spots off suede areas, try
a dribble of alcohol in
mild detergent suds.
Apply the froth with a
stiff brush, wipe with a
damp sponge, let dry,
and go over with a stiff
dry sponge to lift the
nap.**

SUGGESTIONS

- To extend the life of clothes with elastic, dry only until the *fabric* is dry. Then hang out until elastic dries.
- Quick-drying fabrics overdry in a matter of minutes. It's a good idea to put a damp (not wet) towel in with them unless you are there to remove them as soon as they dry. The towel prolongs drying time by adding more moisture. Keep drying time short, however—10 to 15 minutes. This works well with coin-operated dryers, since they are often so hot they dry much too quickly.
- If you pay attention to temperature settings, prevent overcrowding, and don't overdry, you should get fluffy, smooth, nonclingy results. Fabric softeners, in most cases, won't be necessary.

For *average* drying times, see the chart below. Remember that a mixed load will take longer, particularly if it contains heavy cottons (towels, for instance); so will a large load.

AVERAGE DRYING TIMES

FABRIC	TIME (MINUTES)	CYCLE
acetate/triacetate	20	Low or Permanent Press
acrylic/modacrylic/all lightweight man-mades	15	Low or Permanent Press
cotton—thin	30	Permanent Press or Regular
cotton—heavy	45 (or more)	Regular
linen—thin	15–20	Permanent Press (to be ready for ironing, they should still be quite damp)
linen—heavy	25	Permanent Press (to be ready for ironing, they should still be quite damp)
polycotton	30	Permanent Press

LINE DRYING

This old-fashioned standby saves money and wear and tear on clothes. Items such as synthetic socks and underwear last a lot longer if they aren't exposed to dryer heat.

The following items are good candidates for line drying:

- clothes so labeled
- clothes to be ironed
- things you don't want to shrink
- any knit not labeled "Tumble Dry"
- clothes containing elastic, like noncotton socks and underwear
- fabrics bonded to a backing
- nylon/spandex blends
- well-worn clothes

Nylon line is practical because it can be wiped clean with a household spray, but a cotton line can be washed with soap and water. For indoor drying, the easiest to manage is a roll-out line installed over the tub or in any bright warm spot where drips don't matter. (A sturdy, stable folding rack is sometimes even more practical.) Line drying maintains the shape of the garment as it dries.

- Dry delicate items such as thin polyester blouses on rustproof hangers.
- To prevent marks when clothes are draped over a line or bar, put a towel or two underneath.
- For most line drying, hang things from the hem, upside down, rather than from the shoulders, since the hem is usually the widest part and clothespin marks aren't as obvious there. The point is to distribute the weight evenly.
- Hang pleated no-iron skirts (usually nylon, acrylic, or polyester) from the waist, securing them evenly across the top. That way the pleats fall into place. This is also the best way to hang a very full skirt, although you may have to iron it a bit.
- Smooth and pull clothes to shape as you hang them up; it saves ironing and folding time later.
- The sun tends to bleach colors. If you are drying clothes outdoors, set the line where clothes get direct sun briefly or not at all, or remove clothes as soon as they're dry. You can also dry colored items inside out, particularly cottons, linens, and rayon. Of course if you do want to bleach cottons and linens white, leave them to dry in direct sun.
- To fluff line-dried towels, simply run on low or no heat for a few minutes in the dryer before line drying.

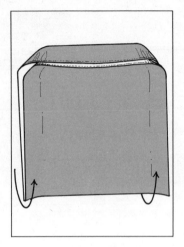

6. Folding

- The only way to fold clothes neatly is to lay them on a clean, nonslippery, preferably slightly cushioned surface, then pat them smooth and pull gently to shape before folding.
- Pull side seams straight so they lie parallel, if possible. Then smooth. For trousers, match the inseam and the outseam on both legs, then lay flat and smooth with the hand.
- To minimize creases, make as few folds as possible, wherever possible matching the shape of the folded item to your drawer or shelf space. Rolling rather than folding works well with many clothes, particularly knits.

TO FOLD A FITTED SHEET
- Fold in half, bringing the shorter ends together. Turn the two ears at one end inside out so they fit over their opposite numbers.
- Fold in half again, so that the four ears meet at one corner. Turn one *pair* of ears inside out so they fit under the other pair.
- Lay flat, smooth, and arrange the side pieces neatly. Fold to a convenient size.

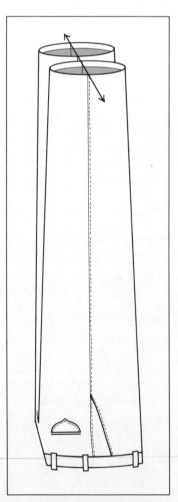

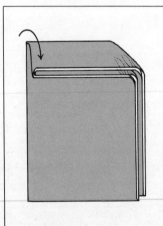

WHITER, BRIGHTER, AND SOFTER ——

BLEACHING

Chlorine bleaching oxidizes, or burns off, dirt and dyes. It also disinfects. (It should be used selectively. Labels may say "No Bleach" or "No Chlorine Bleach"; see the Fiber Treatment Chart for exceptions.) If colors are fast, chlorine bleach can be used in small quantities in the wash, but only occasionally.

For whitening or brightening general wash, first, be sure you're using enough detergent in the wash to get it clean. Next, turn first to the suggestions for presoaking on page 55. For whites and pastels you might try bluing (on cotton, linen, rayon, or wool) or a detergent containing optical brighteners (on synthetics).

If you still aren't satisfied, try chlorine bleaching with fabrics that can take it:

- Be sure clothes are colorfast, as this is a strong chemical. For general laundry use, follow the directions on the bottle, putting a measured amount in a machine dispenser. The dispenser is timed to open partway through the wash cycle, so that soap or detergent has a chance to work first and to dilute the bleach so that it won't create spots on wet clothes.
- If you have no dispenser, mix ¼ cup of chlorine bleach well with 2 cups of warm water (double this for large-capacity washers; cut it in half for small loads and in areas with soft water). Add this solution to the washing machine after 5 to 7 minutes of wash time or during the first rinse cycle, once the rinse water is in. If possible, have the machine agitating while you add the solution. Try to pour it into the wash or rinse water rather than directly onto the clothes. Add a couple of tablespoons of plain vinegar to the *last* rinse to chemically neutralize any chlorine bleach residues. Then give an extra rinse, if possible.

NOTE: For a slow, gentle presoak to perk up yellowed fabrics (check the Fiber Treatment Chart if in doubt about a fiber) and to disinfect diapers, use a solution of

    1 tablespoon of chlorine bleach.
    1 gallon of water.
    2 tablespoons of borax.

Soak up to 1 hour, then rinse well and neutralize as above. This is also useful for freshening dishcloths or sponges and for disinfecting a sick person's clothes.

SUGGESTIONS
- Don't mix ammonia and chlorine bleach; this releases toxic fumes.
- Don't mix chlorine bleach directly with soap, detergent, laundry boosters, enzyme presoaks, fabric softeners, or bluing, as this renders them ineffective.
- Never use bleach on clothes labeled "Dry Clean Only" even if you're washing them.
- Sunlight is nature's way of bleaching white cotton and linen. Use it whenever possible instead of chlorine bleach.

BLUING AND BRIGHTENERS

Bluing and synthetic optical whiteners trick the human eye into seeing a whiter white or a brighter pastel. Bluing, which is best added in the last rinse, can be bought in various forms. Synthetic optical whiteners, substitutes for bluing formulated for polyester, nylon, and other fibers that don't absorb much water, are usually found premixed with a detergent.

Bluing can be a good substitute for whitening by chlorine bleaching; it is *not* a substitute for getting clothes clean. It is most effective on fabrics that readily absorb water such as cotton, linen, and rayon but can be used with all machine-washables. Here's how to use bluing most effectively:
- Follow directions on the container except where the instructions say to add to the wash cycle. Add it to the last *rinse* cycle instead.
- To use bluing in a sink or laundry tub, follow package directions. Add ½ teaspoon of salt to prevent streaking. Be sure to shake clothes out before adding them to the solution. Do only 1 or 2 pieces at a time and swish them back and forth continuously by hand or with a long-handled implement. *Never leave them to soak. Don't leave them to drain in the sink,* as this can cause streaking. Lift them out, squeeze them gently, and rinse once. Lay them out flat on dry towels and roll to extract water.
- If you've overblued:
  — Rinse clothes that can stand hot water in *very* hot water, stirring in a few tablespoons of washing soda or heavy-duty detergent. Wash and rinse until you remove the bluing.

— Rinse more delicate fabrics in cool water and proceed as above.
• If you've spilled bluing, rinse with lots of warm or hot water with 2 tablespoons of plain vinegar added. If this doesn't work, rub some laundry bar soap into the stain. Bleach as a last resort.

FABRIC SOFTENERS

Soap has a natural softening action, but detergents, which are now used for most washing, don't. That's why the demand for fabric softeners has risen.

The most generally available products are liquids, used in the last rinse, and sheets, used in the dryer. Washer-added softeners penetrate fabric better and therefore produce fluffier results; dryer-added softeners do a good job at reducing static cling.

Many softeners produce a gradual coating that can make stain-removal difficult and fabric look dingy. The remedy is to use them occasionally rather than in every wash. If you pay attention to temperature settings, avoid overcrowding, and don't overdry, you can cut down on your need for fabric softeners. Here are more suggestions for their use:
• Use fabric softeners only when clothes are clean, adding it in the rinse cycle even if the box says that you can use it right in the wash.
• *Remove* sheets from the dryer after each use.
• Never pour liquid softener directly on clothes. Dilute with water before adding by hand.
• Don't use bluing at the same time as you use fabric softener.
• If liquid softener seems to have left stains, wash the article thoroughly by hand, using laundry bar soap and water.

SUGGESTIONS
• Since fabric softeners can build up and give clothes a slippery feel, you may want to avoid them. Problems of static cling and stiffness can be solved by
— increasing the amount of soap or detergent in the regular wash.
— making sure the water is soft enough.
— removing clothes from the dryer as soon as they are dry.

• Finally, let us stress that one key to success is to do laundry from start to finish whenever possible. You'll be more attentive to such things as sorting and drying time, which make all the difference in the results you get.

WASHING BY HAND

Handwashing is an easy way to do a few items, and certainly the best method for lingerie, wool sweaters, washable silks, and a host of other clothes. It is very practical for a small wardrobe and is the best way to prolong the life of a piece of clothing.

Observe "Handwash" labels! Handwashing is vital for clothes, fabric, and/or dyes that cannot take the stress and strain of machine agitation and spin. Although dry cleaning may be suggested on the label, many items—polyester, nylon, acrylic, and cashmere, for example—are better off handwashed.

You can of course also handwash anything labeled "Machine Wash," and might be advised to do so if you are concerned about durability.

Good items to handwash even if not so labeled are

• clothes that contain spandex, or elastic.
• clothes with rubber content, such as slickers.
• sheer stockings and lingerie.
• permanent-pleated synthetics.
• clothes with lace inserts—these tend to pull free.

Here is a general procedure to follow when handwashing anything:

1. Before you wash anything the first time, test it for colorfastness. Zip zippers, button buttons, etc.
2. Run a *generous* sinkful (most bathroom sinks hold 2 to 2½ gallons) of water—cool or barely warm to the hand. Soften hard water with about ½ tablespoon of borax, or use distilled water. If the fabric has a long or fluffy nap, be sure there's enough water so the clothes float freely.
3. Dissolve well 1 capful or 2 teaspoons of mild soap or detergent to make suds. Since concentration varies from product to product, aim for good but not thick suds. If you overdo, remember to reduce the amount the next time around. *Optional:* To remove oily soil

from synthetics and durable press, add 1 tablespoon of ammonia to the suds.

4. Check for and gently remove stains. Lots of ordinary soil will come out if rubbed with laundry bar soap. You can use a soft nailbrush to get at stains but only on smooth, firm fabrics. *Keep the fabric moist.* Dry rubbing damages yarns. If the material has a long or fluffy nap, soak any stain with an appropriate liquid cleaning agent.

5. Do only a few articles at a time. Submerge till *thoroughly saturated* with suds. Then squeeze suds through gently—no twisting or wringing—for two minutes or so. *Don't leave to soak.* If suds subside, remove the clothes and make more suds.

   If the fabric has a long or fluffy nap, strip the soapy water out by holding the material with one hand and stripping gently with the other thumb and forefinger in a gentle downward motion so as not to stretch the fabric or tangle the nap.

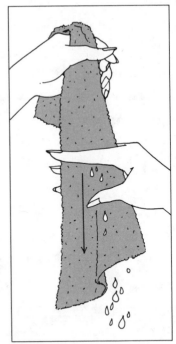

STRIPPING

6. Drain the water from the sink, then *press the clothes to extract the water* rather than lifting them out of the sink. A gallon of water weighs over 8 pounds, and its weight can easily drag delicate fabrics out of shape.

7. Fill sink and repeat *until the rinse water stays clear.* Twice should be enough if you haven't overdone the soap.

8. Now lay each article flat on a dry towel or between two towels (put one inside, too, if there's any danger of color running). *Stretch and pat gently to shape,* especially collars, cuffs, seams, and hems. Roll up, pressing to extract more water. *The more often you roll in dry towels, the shorter the drying time will be.* Put to dry flat or on a rack or line or on rustproof hangers. *To prevent line, hanger, or rack marks, pad with several towels.*

   If the fabric has a long or fluffy nap, you will get the best results if you pat out carefully to shape on one towel, then put another on top. Change to dry towels several times while drying, turning the article each time so the long hairs dry evenly. A net sweater dryer allows air to circulate, which speeds drying. Straighten fringe yarns several times during drying. When *nearly dry,* shake out to fluff.

All these considerations may seem a bit overwhelming in the beginning, but if you concentrate first on the six fundamental steps, then use the information on specific methods as you need them, they will quickly become thoroughly familiar.

FOREIGN CARE LABELS

30°C	Wash cool.	⊗	Do not dry clean.
40°C			
60°C	Wash warm.	↑ (in circle)	Dry clean.
75°C	Wash in hot water.	P (in circle)	Dry clean, but not with trichloroethylene type; usual cleaner's "perc" fine.
3 / 60°C	Wash three times (or number given) separately at temperature indicated to get rid of surface dye.	F (in circle)	Dry clean with petroleum or fluorocarbon solvents only.
⊠ (triangle)	No chlorine bleach.	▱	Hang to dry.
Do not wash.	Do not wash.	|||	Hang wet to drip dry.
Iron (one dot)	Iron low or low steam setting.	—	Dry flat.
Iron (two dots)	Iron medium settings.		
Iron (three dots)	Iron cotton or linen setting.		
Iron (crossed out)	Do not iron.		

NOTE: If colors are used, red means *don't*, amber means *proceed with caution*, and green means *go*.

FIBER TREATMENT CHART

Here is your guide for deciding how to treat colorfast clothes. Consider all information on care labels as well as the table below.

	CHLORINE BLEACH OCCASIONALLY	HOT WATER WASH OCCASIONALLY	CAN BE WHITENED	CAN TAKE ALKALINE CLEANERS*	USE SOAP OR DISHWASHING LIQUID	USE REGULAR OR HEAVY DUTY DETERGENT
Acetate/Triacetate	No	No	No	No	Yes	No
Acrylic/Modacrylic	No	Yes	No	Only occasionally	Yes	Yes
Cotton (tough)†	Yes	Yes	Yes	Yes	Yes	Yes
Linen/Ramie (tough)	Yes	Yes	Yes	Yes	Yes	Yes
Lurex	No	No	No	No	Yes	Yes, okay for fiber in blend
Nylon (tough)	Yes	Yes	Yes	Only occasionally	Yes	Yes
Olefin	No	No	No	No	Yes	Yes
Permanent Press	No	Yes	No	Only occasionally	Yes	Yes
Polyester (tough)	If all else fails	Yes	No	Yes	Yes	Yes
Rayon	If all else fails	No	Possibly	No	Yes	No
Silk	No	No	No	No	Yes	No
Spandex	No	No	No	No	Only occasionally	No
Stretch Fabrics	No	Yes	Maybe	Only occasionally	Yes	Yes
Wool	No	No	No	No	Yes	No

*This category includes ammonia, automatic dishwasher detergent, liquid hard-surface household cleaners, and laundry booster products. Chlorine bleach and heavy-duty detergents are also highly alkaline, but they are listed on the chart because they are used more frequently.
†Treat fine cottons as rayons.

CHAPTER FOUR

Pressing Matters

You're standing over your son's button-down cotton shirt wondering why it still looks rumpled after all your efforts. What to do? Before trying to improve your technique, size up your equipment. A good ironing board, sleeveboard, and iron make all the difference to ironing results. The investment up front may seem a bit steep, but sturdy, well-made equipment lasts for years and the pleasure of getting good results is worth more than you may realize.

Professional-quality equipment is best. You may have to hunt a little for it, but there are usually commercial outlets in large cities; some hardware and housewares stores carry the right stuff. The problem with garden-variety equipment is that it is often so flimsy it's almost useless for the jobs it's meant to do.

Inspect carefully before you buy, taking into consideration the points given below.

WHAT YOU NEED

An Ironing Board: This must be sturdily made, conveniently adjustable to different heights, and *absolutely* stable. Be sure it has rubber caps on the feet. Then prepare it properly. Secure enough padding to make a firm but somewhat resilient layer about half an inch thick. Old blankets, cotton flannel, or store-bought precut pads will do. A piece of the "silence cloth" used under tablecloths is ideal. Any of these porous fabrics speed drying because steam passes through them and evaporates. You can pin or sew the fabric in place.

Cover the pad with a single layer of felt or cotton flannel and secure it underneath with heavy thread or lengths of binding tape sewn to either side so they can be tied. *Before* sewing the ties on, pin them in place, then check to see that the board opens and shuts easily.

The final layer is either a piece of white sheet or of fine white linen (coarser weaves will leave impressions on thin materials) or a prepackaged silicone-treated cover, which discourages scorching and sticking. (A plain cover is a good choice, as it doesn't distract when you're ironing sheer fabric.) Whichever cover you choose, it should be removable for occasional washing. To finish, pin any hanging covering material carefully up out of the way.

To set your ironing board up, pick a site where you have room to move around and one that gets good light. If you're *right-handed,* the nose—for most work—should be on your *left.* The board should be at a comfortable height for putting weight down on the iron. One way to find the right height for you is to adjust the board until you can stand with your arms straight and your hand flat on the board.

A Sleeveboard: This is invaluable for shaping small areas like armholes, doing curved seams, ironing children's clothes, and giving a crease-free press to sleeves, cuffs, and trousers. It is worth the investment—about $25.00—if it's solidly made. The best are reversible, having two narrow but somewhat differently shaped boards to fit many varied clothing designs. Put some padding under the cover that should come with it. Only one layer of thick and one layer of thinner padding is needed.

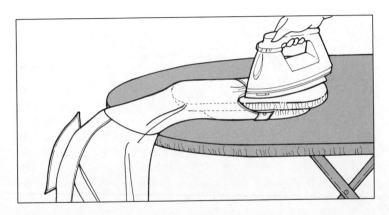

To remove burrs from metal soleplates, use a damp cork dipped in gentle abrasive cleanser. Rinse, then set iron on low heat and run over waxed paper or rub lightly with beeswax.

An Iron: These come with all sorts of added attractions, but the most useful features are as follows:

- *adequate weight.* Get the heaviest you can—3½ pounds is probably the maximum nowadays.
- *an aluminum soleplate.* A coated bottom is optional, and sewing supply stores sell a slip-on shoe as an alternative. With a coated bottom you won't need to use a presscloth, but it will scratch eventually.
- *good steam output.* This *isn't* a matter of the number of holes in the sole but of steam output and pressure. An extra-steam or surge-of-steam feature *is* useful, however. Be sure that the release button isn't easy to press inadvertently, as steam can scald badly.
- *a wide, clearly marked temperature/fabric range.* Different makes vary widely in actual range; Wool can be 340°F, or as high as 425°. As an iron ages, it heats less reliably, too. Only the manufacturer knows for sure. A range of 120° to 450° is optimum. Write the company to find out, call their Customer Service Department, or look it up in a consumer guide. *With a new iron, use slightly lower settings until you know how it performs*—for example, set at Cotton when ironing linen.

Before you use your iron, unclog the steam holes. If there is a self-cleaning feature, use it, or simply set the iron on Steam and run it over a spare piece of cloth; another possibility is to wipe out each hole with a slightly damp cotton swab trimmed to fit.

To get gummy accumulations off, wipe the cool iron with a cloth dipped in a solution of ammonia and water, or use Glass Wax. Keeping the iron free of starch or other buildup prevents stains when ironing.

Other Equipment

A Pump-spray Bottle: For dampening clothes. It should have an adjustable spray for convenience. Fill it with distilled water.

12-by-18-inch Presscloths: For protecting clothes from excessive heat. Thin, absorbent materials such as tea towels suit thin fabrics: thicker ones such as wool scraps suit thicker fabrics. Brown wrapping paper is easy to use because it is stiff and slips easily under pleats and facings.

A Press Pad: For extra cushioning under buttons and other trim. Thick felt works well.

A Needleboard: Optional. This is a specialty item and is used to keep velvet and other plush fabrics from being crushed during ironing. You can substitute a clean piece of pile carpeting or of velvet, corduroy, or similar fabric.

A Hook and Lightweight Chain: For steadying a dress while pleats are ironed.

A Portable Rod: For convenience in hanging up freshly ironed clothes.

You should also keep the following common household supplies on hand:

- sponges, for dampening small areas.
- spray-on fabric sizing: starch or the lighter "fabric finish."
- waxed paper (or beeswax), for smoothing the iron.
- pins, to anchor slippery materials and block knits.
- hangers, for different kinds of clothes.
- brown wrapping paper, for use as a substitute presscloth.
- hand lotion, for keeping your skin moist.

IMPROVING YOUR IRONING TECHNIQUE ————————————

Problems usually come from not having the right combination of pressure, heat, and moisture.

Pressure is applied either by true ironing—moving the iron back and forth over flat areas—or by pressing an up-down-press-then-lift motion used for defining the basic shape of a garment and for doing detail work such as darts and pleats. ALWAYS wiggle the iron a little when pressing so that it doesn't leave a mark! You should also press rather than iron where the back-and-forth rubbing of ironing would create shine. Since pressing gives the basic outline to clothes, do it *before* ironing.

Let the weight of the iron create the pressure; you don't need to lean on it.

Heat relaxes fibers. The iron settings can be your guide, but use the coolest setting that will do the job, since heat also ages cloth fibers: try one step below the standard mark, for example. Because heat fades many colors, work on the reverse of a fabric whenever possible, particularly with bright colors.

Moisture also relaxes fibers. Some fabrics need only the steam from a steam iron; others should be dampened before you begin ironing.

Absolutely-don't-irons: Plasticized fabrics, rubber, spandex, olefin (polypropylene). And go easy with anything elasticized—iron only with a presscloth or other fabric over the elastic.

Wool rescue: If you press in shine, dab on a solution of 1 tablespoon of plain vinegar and 1 cup of cool water with a sponge. Then steam the area well to swell the flattened fibers.

Here's a quick moisture gauge for ironing:
ACETATE—steam-iron.
ACRYLIC/MODACRYLIC—steam-iron.
BLENDS—as you would predominant fiber.
COTTON—evenly damp.
DURABLE PRESS—steam-iron.
LINEN—very damp.
NYLON—steam-iron.
POLYESTER—steam-iron.
RAYON—slightly damp or steam-iron.
SILK—evenly damp (only *washable* silks), or steam iron.
TRIACETATE—steam-iron.
WOOL—steam-iron or mist lightly.

NEVER USE A DRY IRON ON DRY FABRIC. Moisture protects against scorching, glazing, melting, shriveling, and fading of dyes.

You can provide moisture in one of four ways:
- Using a steam iron (preferably filled with distilled water). All synthetics should iron up well on a Steam or Permanent Press/Steam setting. Be sure acrylic/modacrylic and acetate are on a *low* steam setting, however. Steam ironing is also good for most touch-ups.
- Using a damp presscloth between fabric and iron. The iron should be on a Dry setting in this case. This is especially handy for touching up small areas like the back of a linen blouse. Once the area is dampened, remove the cloth and iron or press until the clothes are dry. (A neat trick for travelers: dampen a washcloth or hand towel and use as a presscloth.)
- Ironing or pressing while the clothes are still damp *or* sprinkling or spraying thoroughly with water, then folding or rolling the clothes up neatly and firmly for at least 15 minutes while the water travels along the fibers. This is most effective with linen and cotton. Iron with a dry iron.
- Spraying sizing on dry fabric. This is most effective on the absorbent fibers—cotton, linen, silk, rayon, and wool. Iron with a dry iron.

Clothes that don't respond well to steam ironing need either sprinkling and rolling or spray-on sizing. (Clothes that you want to look starched need sizing, too, of course.)

The best combination for many clothes is to dampen them, then iron or press, and finish with a light spray-sizing and ironing.

For wool, silk, durable press, heavyweight polyester, and polycotton the Wool or a fairly high Permanent Press setting should work well. Use steam unless the fabric is damp. When ironing wool on the front, prevent shine by pressing through a slightly damp presscloth.

IRONING DO'S AND DON'TS ——————

SOME DO'S

- Always experiment cautiously on an inconspicuous area until you know how a new item performs. Review Chapter 12 for specific suggestions and warnings.
- A good routine is to first press seams, then areas such as darts, since these give clothes their basic shape. Next do other detailing, such as sleeves and collars, and finally the flat ironing.
- You must press, and later iron, *with the grain* of the material—that is, along the warp threads. This is almost always top to bottom, although bias-cut clothes are put together on the diagonal. Look at the weave.
- Both pressing and flat ironing will take better, especially with dampened clothes, if you leave the section you've just finished in place while you count to 15 and fan it with your hand to help evaporate the last bit of moisture. It also helps to set the press if you hang the clothes up in an airy spot on a properly shaped hanger for 10 minutes or so before putting them away.
- If cuffs, plackets, and other places where there are two layers of fabric don't iron up smooth, try dampening well or spraying with sizing.
- For greater stiffness, don't just spray on large quantities of sizing. Spray lightly and evenly, iron or press, then repeat until you get the results you want. Use moderate heat, as sizing can scorch. (Remove scorch by brushing it off, and if that doesn't work, presoak in water with a little vinegar added, then wash.)
- If sizing produces white flakes on clothes, shake the can more vigorously, rinse the spray nozzle to unclog it, and be sure the fabric you're working with is absorbent enough. Many synthetics aren't absorbent, so sizing simply stays on the surface. *Never* use sizing near an open flame.
- Go slowly on both stretchy and crisp fabrics, pressing where possible, to avoid unwanted creases, which can be difficult to remove.

Baggy knees in a wool suit? You can use hot steam to eliminate bagginess—no presscloth, no pressing, just let steam from the iron, held an inch or so above the fabric, penetrate well. Leave for a few minutes, then iron lightly from top to bottom—that is, along the warp threads— unless clothes are cut on the bias.

- Iron linings, lowering the temperature if necessary. It does make a difference in how the clothes look.
- If you switch from steam to dry ironing, lift the iron to let steam blow off for a minute.
- Since ironing decreases a fabric's absorbency, you may not want to iron such things as sheets and towels.

SOME DON'TS

- Never iron over areas where there might be perspiration or other stains.
- Avoid pulling on material and seams while ironing as it often results in puckers when the fabric contracts after you release it.
- Never iron over pins or other protruding objects. Work around them or press face down on a padded board.
- Never iron down hemlines and other folds harshly.
- Never iron with the tip pointed down when using steam—it can spill scalding water.

PRESSING PROBLEMS ――――――――

Good results depend not only on the right combination of heat, moisture, and pressure but also on the knowledge of how to handle various kinds of detailing.

Bias-cut Clothes

- The grain of the fabric is on the diagonal, to give fluidity, rather than the usual up and down. Since the fabric sags and stretches easily, press rather than iron—especially hems and seams—working *with* the diagonal yarns.

Collars

- Stretch flat, then press the band, if any, first.
- Press the underside, working perpendicular to the edge with the tip of the iron to prevent wrinkles.

Cuffs

- Open them flat and iron the inside first, working from the hem toward the seam attaching the cuff to the shirt. Treat French cuffs as collars, but finish by tamping the iron gently along the inside of the fold to set it.

Darts

- Darts provide three-dimensional shaping, so don't iron them flat: press the wide part just to the point, using the tip of the iron rather than flattening the whole area.
- Slip brown paper between the dart and the underlying fabric if the material is thin.

If the hem of a favorite wool has stretched way out of shape, don't call it quits! Run a basting thread parallel to the hem edge and pull tight enough so the hem has the right dimensions. Then let hot steam penetrate very thoroughly, using the highest steam setting. Leave to dry, then remove basting thread.

Elastic Waistbands

- All elastic should be ironed in a test area first to make sure it can withstand heat without losing its elasticity.
- If it passes the test, stretch it around the ironing board so you can iron the fabric casing smooth. Use the lowest heat that is effective.

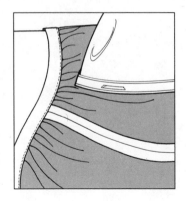

Facings

- If you iron or press facings separately, the edge won't leave a mark on the front of the clothes. Slip brown paper between the two layers of material if you can, or slip the iron underneath to press the outer fabric, then turn over and slip it in to iron the facing itself.

Gathers and Shirring

- Shirring is simply very small gathers. Do either one on the reverse. Lift the material that gathers the fabric— a waistband, for example—with your free hand, then zigzag *slowly and gently* in and out with the tip of the iron. This will give you a soft, professional finish. The smaller the gathers and the more slippery the material, the more often you will have to shift the garment. Press the waistband separately and, to finish, run the tip of the iron along the seam that holds the gathers.
- Press a seam allowance on the underside *away* from the gathers.

Hems

- Press on the inside first, then touch up the outside gently. It is better simply to steam wool and wool blends, then gently tamp with a wooden block or an old book. For a firmer shape for wools, use a dry press-cloth and steam-press.
- Rolled hems should be ironed on the right side so as to run less risk of breaking the stitching. Iron *parallel* to the rolled hem.
- For other very shallow hems, smooth the area you're working on flat and run the iron parallel to the hem edge.

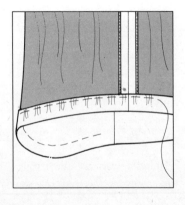

Plackets

- Work with the grain of the placket, which may not be the same as the surrounding fabric. To give a neat finish, use the tip of the iron to crisp the edges.
- Since plackets are made of two layers of fabric, you may get better results if you start with them quite damp, then press till they're *dry*, or simply use spray-on sizing.

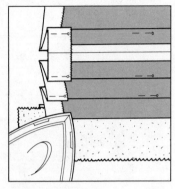

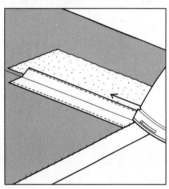

Pleats
- There are two kinds of pleats: zigzag—the narrowest are called crystal pleats—and box, of which kick pleats are a common example.
- To get them to hang evenly, you must first press the underneath folds, then the outer ones. Position them carefully, pinning at top and bottom if necessary, particularly with permanent press.
- To prevent impressions, slip strips of brown paper or cardboard—for heavier fabrics—into the folds.
- To make things easier when you're ironing the pleated skirt of a dress, put a hanger in the bodice and attach it to a nearby chair with a light hook and chain.

Pockets
- First press the inside of the pocket separately. (With patch pockets, cut cardboard to shape and slip inside while pressing.)
- Now press along the edge with the tip of the iron.
- When a pocket is set into a seam, be sure to align the edge neatly with the seamline *before* pressing.

Ruffles
- Treat ruffles as you would gathers. For a neat finish, use the tip of the iron to press the join where the ruffle is attached.

Seams
- Smooth seams flat, but to prevent puckering, don't stretch them while ironing.
- Iron the length of a seam, not across it, pressing curved seams over a suitable shape. Do the inside, pressing open seams open and bound seams to one side, usually to the back. Use brown paper under the seam allowances to prevent impressions. Now press on the outside, using a presscloth where necessary to prevent shine.

Sleeves
- Do any lining first, then such details as gathers at the shoulders. You will first use the tip of the iron to press *toward* the seam on the body of the garment, then shape the armhole seam as for curved seams. A sleeveboard is handy here.
- Do the flat areas last, using rolled towels to get a rounded shape if you don't have a sleeveboard. Finish by pressing the cuff gently with the tip of the iron perpendicular to it.

- To do puffed sleeves, stuff with towels, steam, and press gently, then leave the toweling in while the press sets. If you like, stuff with tissue paper to store.

Tailoring
- See pages 120–21.

Tucks
- Treat tucks as you would darts. Some tucks have the fold inside, some outside. Work on the side the fold is on.
- Press along the stitching, just to the end where the fabric is released. Then press the flat areas around the tuck up to where the stitching begins.

Waistbands (nonelastic)
- This is a finishing touch: Press lengthwise, rotating the band around the nose of the board. Do the inside first.
- Then use the tip of the iron to crisp any details set into the waist (pleats or gathers, for example), working at right angles to the waistband. Finally, press along the seam with the edge of the iron.
- Where there are buttons, work on the reverse. Cushion them with a padding of extra towels unless your board is already well cushioned.

Zippers
- You may want to do the zipper last, since the several layers of fabric involved take longer to dry and you will get better results if these are nearly dry when you begin pressing.
- The iron should never touch the zipper itself. First close the zipper and press the inside flaps, with the garment inside out, using the tip of the iron. (If it isn't damp enough, steam or spray with sizing to get it flat.) Hold the zipper taut while pressing.
- Now open the zipper and press lightly along the fabric in which it is set.
- Close it again and press the outer covering. Use a presscloth to prevent shine.

NOTE: If a zipper was set in improperly in the first place or if the stitching has shrunk during washing, it will not iron flat. The only cure is to have a new zipper put in by a skilled tailor or seamstress.

A last suggestion: Keep the ironing board and iron set up if you have the space. (Do not set up in an area where children play.) Nothing makes it easier to get to a pile of ironing or a last-minute touch-up.

CHAPTER FIVE

You and Your Dry Cleaner

A good job of dry cleaning depends essentially on that increasingly rare breed, the careful, competent dry cleaner. Even when the proprietor has tried to train his staff well and holds them to high standards, you will still often have to deal with many frustrating problems.

But take heart. Armed with the information in this chapter you should be able to zero in on the best available cleaner *and* get the best possible service.

WHAT MUST BE DRY CLEANED . . . AND WHAT NEEDN'T BE

Why is it that many clothes are labeled "Dry Clean Only" when they appear to be colorfast and the fabric itself is washable—a corduroy, for instance?

Part of the answer is that manufacturers often put only the most foolproof method of cleaning on the label. Turning over to the dry cleaner an item that would need special care in washing removes the risk that you, the buyer, will botch the laundering job and make a claim. Current labeling laws don't require that the cheaper alternative, laundering, be given on the label as well.

But it's also true that although the fabric may be washable, the construction of the garment or a finish put on the fabric might not stand up to soap and water or to the agitation of washing.

You *must* dry clean all clothes with the following characteristics:

- Dyes that would run in water—watch especially for prints and other multicolors and for contrasting trim.

- Complicated construction, elaborate or delicate trim, or use of two or more fabrics in the same garment (they might react differently to washing).
- Sheer and other delicate fabrics, particularly those like silk organza where water-soluble sizing holds the yarns in place. When in doubt check Chapter 12 under the name of the fabric.
- Silk clothes labeled "Dry Clean Only" unless (1) the fabric guide listing (e.g. honan) says washing is possible and (2) the garment doesn't pass the washability test on p. 16.
- Tailored clothes—most are wool. These have been shaped and contoured by pressing, and the press would be lost during washing.
- Natural-fiber fabrics using crimped and bouclé yarns such as pebbly-surfaced crepes and chenille. They would uncrimp in washing and either shrink or stretch badly. Also natural-fiber fabrics (and rayon or acetate) that have pressed-in pleats since they aren't permanent as they are in synthetics.
- Any garment with difficult or large stains.
- Unlabeled clothes of wool, rayon, or another fiber not normally washed.

CAUTION: ALWAYS dry clean clothes labeled "Dry Clean Only" the first few times.

You might *want* to dry-clean even washable clothes to get a professional resizing and pressing.

Some labels say "Professionally Dry Clean Only." This simply means that you shouldn't use the coin-operated dry-cleaning units found in some laundromats. Incidentally, the term French dry cleaning has no practical meaning today. Nor do cleaners redye clothes anymore.

How to avoid dry cleaning even if the label says "Dry Clean Only"?

The label can be ignored and the item handwashed if it isn't on the list above and it passes the washability test on page 16. Essentially you must be sure (1) it is color-fast; (2) it won't stretch or shrink when wet; (3) the texture of the fabric won't be altered by soap and water; and (4) the garment's construction allows washing—for example, a pleated silk must be dry cleaned because washing would remove the pleats, but a pleated polyester *can* be washed because the pleats have been permanently set in. CAUTION: After the item is washed, it *must* be air-dried. Then follow the guidelines on ironing.

Are you sitting on a pile of wrinkled wools? Don't try to press them. They should go to a professional to be pressed carefully *inside and out.* Either a highly recommended dry cleaner or a tailoring concern should be able to do the job properly.

CUTTING DOWN ON CLEANING BILLS

- When you buy clothes that must be dry cleaned, think about how often they will need cleaning. Many wools and silks, for example, can be worn a number of times between cleanings if they are aired out and given a touch-up with the iron. Synthetics and linen, however, need cleaning much more often.
- Buy clothes that fit comfortably. A tight fit stretches clothes out of shape quickly.
- Alternate washing with dry cleaning when that's feasible.
- Air clothes when you take them off. Don't leave them in a heap so that the fibers dry in wrinkles.
- Give your clothes inner support by placing them on properly shaped hangers.
- Don't wear something two days in a row—clothes need a rest between wearings.
- Steam and brush wool and steam silk after wearing.
- Before getting dressed, wipe away skin oils with a mild astringent like witch hazel. Neck and wrists are the prime target areas.

Of course there will be times when you want to dry-clean washable clothes. It's convenient, and the cleaner will give a professional and more lasting press and resizing. But it's a good idea to look up the appropriate entry in the fiber and fabric guides first. Some fibers, such as nylon, don't respond well to dry-cleaning.

While you can often save time and money by avoiding dry-cleaning, you will also need the services of a good dry cleaner from time to time.

FINDING THE BEST DRY CLEANER

Here are the basics:
- Shop around for a clean, friendly establishment where the owner is on hand to take responsibility and where cleaning and finishing are done on the premises. Avoid places with a high staff turnover—good work demands skilled, reasonably contented personnel whom you can get to know.
- Ask whether the owner is a member of the Neighborhood Cleaners Association (NCA) or an equivalent trade organization that keeps cleaners abreast of de-

velopments in their field. You can ask for the NCA's informative pamphlets on new fabrics and services.

- Check the equipment to see that it is well kept even if it is not new. There should be hand irons available for doing detail work.
- Stain removal should be handled carefully. A specialist called a spotter is needed for this. If a spot can't be removed, the clothes should be returned with a tag stating that the cleaner was unable to remove this stain.
- Look for receipts that are legible, giving your name and address, a description of the clothes (though you may have to add to it if "bl.sh." is too vague), the cost of service, and notations of any special work you requested. *Keep your receipts:* they aren't the only means of making a legal claim in case of loss, but they are by far the easiest.
- Pickup and delivery, when offered, should be efficient, and bills should be itemized clearly. Careful packaging and wrapping are important. Plastic clips holding clothes on the hanger are preferable to pins.
- Measuring up to a number of basic standards is a must. There should be
  - no residual solvent smell.
  - no ironed-in wrinkles or harsh creases.
  - no shine or impressions at seams or around buttons, pockets, or pleats.
  - neatly ironed linings.
  - a crisp, neatly pressed shape over all.
  - no graying of white and light colors (only possible if the cleaner takes care to do them separately in very fresh solvent so they can't pick up dyes and soil from other items).
  - willingness to do repairs to pockets, linings, hemlines, etc., sewn in thread the same color as the garment. Do not accept clear nylon thread (some cleaners use it to avoid changing spools).

A qualified dry cleaner knows how important it is to give white and delicate garments some special attention during the cleaning process. Unfortunately, fewer and fewer cleaners have the staff, skill, and real pride in their work to take the necessary trouble. What can you do?

Make your standards clear, politely but firmly. Ask for
- hand-pressed linings, especially in tailored clothes.

Is dry-cleaning fluid harmful to clothes? Opinion is divided. But it's generally felt that it's hard on fibers, especially if the dry cleaner doesn't change it often enough. The most obvious evidence of overused solvent is a strong smell clinging to the clothes.

- foil to protect cloth and decorative buttons during cleaning.
- repair of rips and loose hems *before* cleaning.
- a soft press for pleats, creases, and hemlines.
- *no* crease, just a light steaming, if that's what the clothes need.
- tissue stuffing to prevent wrinkling of such things as full sleeves.
- reblocking a knit to shape.
- pre-washing to remove perspiration before dry cleaning.
- extra-long bags clipped or tied at the bottom to protect long gowns or before summer storage.

Then check to see that your requests have been complied with. It is up to you to work *with* the dry cleaner to get results that suit you. A steady customer will always get better service, but so will someone who is precise about what needs to be done and takes time to discuss it.

Several things will save you a lot of aggravation:

- Inspect clothes before taking them to the cleaner so that you know what special treatment they need.
- Reattach loose buttons and make other small repairs before taking clothes to the cleaner.
- Above all, *look clothes over before leaving the store to catch anything that needs redoing!*

A cleaner can't be expected to work miracles. It's your job to bring clothes in before dirt and stains have aged or become ingrained, to be sure to have all parts of an outfit (a suit, for instance) cleaned at the same time, and to pick clothes up before they have time to get squashed on the cleaner's crowded racks.

WHEN PROBLEMS ARISE ━━━━━━━

There are times when something goes wrong—clothes come back with a stain or even a bleached area you know wasn't there when you took them in, or the dimensions are all wrong.

First try to discuss the problem in a friendly manner even if you're feeling cross. Many mistakes can be corrected with a (free) recleaning, reblocking, or re-pressing.

In case of loss or irretrievably damaged clothes, however, stronger measures may be in order. (Forewarned is forearmed: ask about the cleaner's insurance coverage before you actually have to make a claim.) You'll come out better if you have not only the cleaner's receipt but the sales slip showing the original price of the garment and the date of purchase. The insurer's offer—the adjustment—is usually based on the original cost minus depreciation. Clothes are depreciated 100 percent over one, two, or at most three years.

If you're unhappy with the suggested settlement, you should then ask the NCA or other trade association (if you're dealing with a member cleaner) to arbitrate. If you're still unhappy after arbitration, put your evidence in order and file with the nearest small-claims court (it may be called something slightly different where you live). They will need the sales slip and dry cleaner's receipt (if possible), the record of arbitration with dates of calls and meetings, copies of any letters, and in case of damage, the item in dispute.

COIN-OPERATED CLEANING ▬▬▬▬

Coin-operated machines are found in some laundromats. Since the machine just cleans, pressing will be up to you. Look for a clean, orderly establishment *with staff on hand to hang up and bag clothes for you* after they're cleaned.

The most frequent problem is that the solvent isn't changed often enough. Clothes don't get clean, and can even pick up soil from the dirty solvent. They will smell strongly of the cleaning fluid afterwards. When proper care is taken, however, coin-operated cleaning is very economical, since the cost of pressing is avoided.

Best bets for coin-operated cleaning are simply made clothes you can easily iron yourself. Here are some good examples:

- blankets.
- plain wool sweaters and scarves.
- Simply constructed trousers and skirts in all fabrics.
- blazers and similar unconstructed jackets—that is, jackets without padding or interlining.

Among the items you should *avoid* taking to a coin-operated cleaner are

- tailored clothes.
- sheer and other fragile fabrics or designs.
- whites and pastels.
- 100 percent synthetics.

The bottom line about dry cleaning is this: If you are aware of what makes a good cleaning job and what services your cleaner can provide on request, you and your dry cleaner will make an effective team. If you take the trouble to find a topflight cleaner, he or she can add years to the life of your wardrobe.

CHAPTER SIX

Storing Clothes

Storing clothes on a day-to-day or long-term basis is something most of us don't even want to think about. We're pressed for time and short on space, and the whole thing seems too *complicated*.

Here in a few pages is what you need to know to keep clothes in good shape.

HANG-UPS AND PUT-DOWNS

The first thing to know about closets is *not* to use them immediately after taking your clothes off. A good airing—several hours or overnight—not only allows the moisture most fibers absorb from the body to evaporate but deodorizes as well. (Once in a while turn especially thick fabrics inside out to air.) Either hang up your clothes or smooth them out and lay them flat when you take them off, even if that means draping them over a chair. The point is to give clothes a chance to resume their original shape while the cloth fibers are returning to normal as they dry.

If you have the time, steam your tailored clothes after wearing them, particularly those made of wool and silk, in the bathroom for half an hour or so. Keep a wooden clamp hanger on the inside of the bathroom door. Clothes hung there will steam while you bathe or shower, then air when the window and/or door are open. Nothing deodorizes and gets rid of wrinkles better.

ORGANIZERS ——————————————————

Since your major goal is to keep clothes in good shape *and* easily accessible, acquire plenty of hangers:

- Keep extras in the closet so that you don't become frustrated looking for the empty ones.
- Keep them spaced as far apart as possible to avoid crushing the clothes. Padded and heavy wooden hangers automatically space things out well.
- Keep the press in coats, suits, and other tailored clothes by hanging them on shaped wooden hangers. Although you can drape pants over the bar type hanger, you will get a good automatic pressing if you use wooden clamp hangers, lined with felt or with ridges for good holding power, instead. Skirt width will do for trousers, too, so these are the better buy.
- For lightweight blouses get thickly padded, bowed hangers.
- If you must use wire hangers, leave the cleaner's paper on to guard against rust, or spray with a coat of polyurethane or varnish to be sure they're rustproof. Coat any raw, unfinished wood hangers in the same way while you're at it.

If there's room, whole systems of hanging shelves (which need no hardware) will add lots of space for folded items—gloves, shoes, and even hats. Hanging bags can be zipped closed to keep dust off or for long-term storage.

If your closet is too small to make these ideas feasible, or if you have to share it with another person, consider in this order:

- Cold storage through a reliable dry cleaner. If something has recently been cleaned it need not be re-cleaned for storage as long as it looks fresh and has no stains.
- Trunks and chests (cedar-lined, if possible). Then you can use them as end tables or seats. If they're not decorative enough, cover them with a cheerful fabric skirt.
- Tightly closed, *nonplastic* containers that fit under beds or stack in the top of a closet. (*Up* is better than down because less dust will gather.) Be sure to vacuum the area and the container regularly if it's under a bed.
- Thinning out your wardrobe. What you have left will emerge looking infinitely better when the new season rolls around, and will last longer, if it's not jammed into inadequate storage space.

Many clothes should not be hung up and will soon stretch out of shape if left hanging. Most knits should be shelved, and dresses of soft materials like rayon should be hung by loops attached to the waistband with the bodice folded down over the skirt. For longer storage, stuff with tissue and put in boxes.

Don't torture your clothes! Stay away from hooks. Doorknobs are almost as bad. Use hooks only if the clothes have a loop in the collar for hanging and need no ironing—a down jacket, for example.

CLOSET ETIQUETTE ————

- It's easiest to keep things hanging straight if you button all top buttons.
- Keeping different categories of clothes together simplifies dressing.
- To make a wool suit perky, spray a little air freshener around it after you steam and air it and before putting it away.
- If you want a soft roll to a collar, turn it up, or slip a twist of tissue paper under it.
- Don't hang knits unless they are very tightly knit and in regular use. If you do hang them, fold them once the long way, then drape over hanger bar. Put good crisp white tissue in the fold to guard against a crease. *Never hang silk or rayon jersey.*
- The heavier the clothes, the more inner support they can use. Stuff arms of suits and coats with rolls of paper unless in frequent use.
- Very thin fabrics crease. Stuff lightly with tissue—and ask the dry cleaner to do this, too—to keep them in shape.
- Old pillowcases are ideal for holding small collections of items like mittens. Attach a loop that can go on a convenient hook. Then mark as to content in big letters.
- Handbags that aren't stowed in a drawer should be in a plastic bag on a shelf in the closet, *not* hanging by the strap.
- Linen such as tablecloths can be folded and put in a drawer, but there will be fewer creases if they are folded in only one direction, with tissue in the folds, and draped over a wide hanger. An even better idea is to roll them and other flat articles like quilts on large cardboard mailing tubes that you've first covered with tissue paper.
- A closet can be kept fresh smelling by leaving the door ajar regularly so air circulates.
- You can also put sachets of herbs, a pomander, or a scented odor-absorbing wick or stick in the closet. If you can bring yourself to do it, empty closets completely and wash them with mild suds once or twice a year.

TOP DRAWER ———————————————

Again, don't put your clothes away the moment you slip them off! Air them before putting them in the drawer.

Prevent damage from acids in wood—and snagging on splinters—by lining bureau drawers with good shelf paper. Don't use gummed paper for two reasons: insects are attracted to many glues, and it's much easier to remove loose linings.

Flat drawer storage is always best for anything stretchy like a knit. The looser, softer, and finer a fabric is, the more likely it is to need flat storage—very soft leather clothes need padding with tissue and should be stored flat, for example.

Pat clothes out *flat,* then fold either as usual for a shirt or rolled up neatly. Try to put folds where they won't show when you're wearing the clothes—at the waist, for instance.

- The more lightly you tuck things away, the better they will look when they emerge. Therefore a chest with a lot of shallow drawers is more practical than one with a few deep drawers.
- If you have to stack, lighter things go on top of heavier ones. Very light fabrics—a georgette or chiffon, for instance—keep better if well stuffed with tissue paper.
- Gloves can be kept in an oblong box or wrapped in tissue and stacked.
- Smooth out socks, tights, and ties and roll into a snail shape, though ties can hang on a rack, too, of course. (Roll ties up beginning with the narrow end.)
- Fluffy wools and blends shed. It's like having a cat in your drawer. Keep them in tissue or paper bags, or store separately.
- Once or twice a year remove everything and wipe down with a dust cloth or, if necessary, with a sponge dipped in mild soapsuds.
- Use sachets of dried herbs—scented geraniums have delicious-smelling leaves and are easy to raise indoors. Or store boxes of scented soaps with the clothes.

1: *Hatbox* or stand; glazed paper bags are a fine substitute. 2: *Storage box*, with label showing contents. 3a: Broad-shouldered *coat hanger*; 3b: heavy-duty wooden *jacket hanger*; 3c: *skirt hanger*; 3d: padded *blouse and lightweight clothes hanger*. 4a: Wide *hanging shelf bag* for sweaters; 4b: Narrow *hanging shelf bag* for scarves and gloves. 5: *Tie rack* with lots of spaces. 6: *Wicker basket* for quick access to running gear

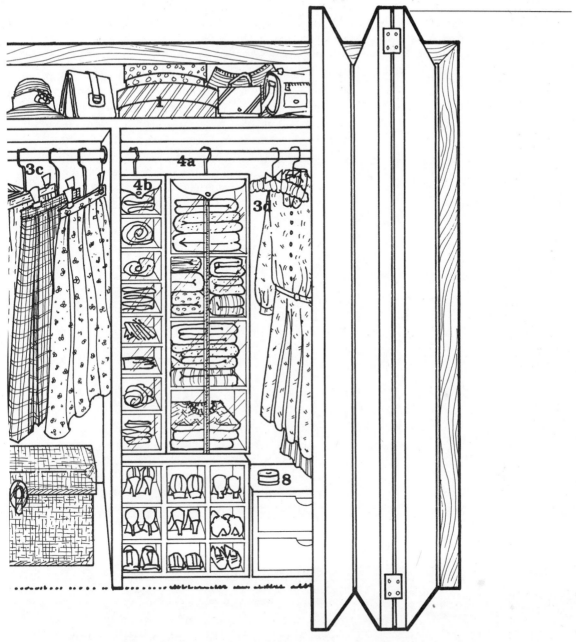

and anything else that needs air and needn't be folded away neatly in the drawer. **7:** *Shoe rack* makes vacuuming the floor easier and keeps shoes in shape. **8:** *Deodorizing wick or stick* by the shoe rack where it's most useful. NOTE: A little luxury is a tall lingerie bureau. Its shallow drawers make it easier to see and reach underwear, stockings, belts, jewelry, and other small items.

LONG-TERM STORAGE ——————————

It's important to prepare both clothes and storage areas in such a way as to prevent conditions that foster bugs, mildew, fading, or the slow corrosion of dust and airlessness. *The best place in which to store clothes is a closet in constant use, since it's easy to monitor and is well ventilated.* But dust will penetrate all the same, so wash after storage unless the clothes look perfectly clean. Below, some cold-storage guidelines for *specific fabrics and items.* Consider *professional* cold storage through a dry cleaner if

- The local climate is very hot (over 75°F) or very humid (over 55 percent humidity regularly).
- You have no place to store things except an unheated, damp basement, or an uninsulated attic that gets too hot and dry in the summer.
- You have furs or fur-trimmed clothes.
- You have chronic problems with carpet beetles, silverfish, moths, or mildew.

The Six-Point Checklist for Long-Term Storage

1. *Stain and chemical protection.* Wash or dry clean each item, removing all stains carefully, since they attract bugs and other animal life. Rinse washables in distilled water carefully to remove mineral and detergent residues. Then iron clothes neatly. If garments are left wrinkled for a long time it will be hard to get them back in shape. They may also show streaks where fading has occurred. DON'T use starch or fabric finish, since it encourages mildew, and many bugs, including moths, find it appetizing.
2. *Moth and insect prevention.* This is only really necessary if you think insects might be a problem and if you are using closed containers. (Signs of insects are dead bugs, webs, or damage to clothes in storage.) Hang a few cedar bags or herbal or eucalyptus sachets among the clothes in open closets. In closed storage, use the familiar and noxious mothball—paradichlorobenzene—in block, flake, or ball form. Suspend above clothes—old stockings are good for this—or strew on layers of paper so they're not in direct contact with clothes. The rule of thumb is 1 pound per

100 cubic feet—say, 8 feet by 4 feet by 3 feet. Replace when the mothballs and their smell have evaporated. *Never put mothballs in direct contact with clothes, and don't use with leather, feathers, or any of the synthetics.* CAUTION: Mothballs are not good for your health. Avoid when possible. If you find there are problems with cockroaches or silverfish, empty the closet or container and wash it. For large infestations, get an exterminator, or spray surfaces with an insecticide. Cedar-liners are effective only if the container is almost completely airtight and clothes are moth-free *before* storage. Cedar is moth-*repellent* but won't kill the larvae which do the damage.

3. *Mouse protection.* Mice like cloth fibers for nests. Check closets—and behind nearby furniture—for holes and then promptly block them up. Put some mothballs around, as they also discourage mice.

4. *Temperature stabilization.* Fibers dry up and become fragile with long exposure to temperatures of 75°F or more. Use a temperature gauge to check, and if there's a problem, consider cold storage.

5. *Dust and light protection.* Brush clothes or shake them out, then layer them with tissue and wrap them in more tissue or keep in closed containers so dust can't settle on them and light will not fade colors. When clothes are in a closet in general use it's enough to cover them in sheeting—old cotton shirts are good, too. (Dark-blue tissue is sometimes recommended because it screens out light, but be careful, for if the paper gets wet, the color can run.) If you must use under-the-bed storage, vacuum the container and its surroundings at least once a month.

6. *Mildew prevention.* Mildew thrives in damp, dark places. Don't put clothes away damp, especially cotton, linen, rayon, ramie, and wool. Let them air on a dry, sunny day for a few hours before storing. *Never store clothes in airtight plastic.* It traps moisture and attracts dust. If storage areas seem damp, keep a light bulb burning or put in bags of silica gel or granular calcium chloride or an open quart container of charcoal (*not* the quick-start kind) to absorb humidity. These should not come in contact with clothes and need to be dried out according to package directions or simply by baking in a slow oven for a few hours when they have absorbed moisture.

Acid-free tissue paper and boxes guarantee that heirlooms you've put away will not suffer acid damage. A local museum can usually direct you to a supplier. Two current sources are University Products, P.O. Box 101, South Canal Street, Holyoke, Mass. 01041, and Talas, 213 West 35th Street, New York, N.Y. 10001.

SPECIAL STORAGE TIPS ──────────

Some fabrics need extra protection, and some clothes need professional attention if they are to survive long storage well: .

- Acetates, acrylic and modacrylic, durable press, nylon, olefin, polyester, and spandex, while easily faded by light, are all moth, insect, and mildew resistant. Blends should be treated according to the natural fiber content, if any.

- Wool and silk need moth, mildew, and insect protection, but they also need to breathe. Never put them in airtight containers. Before storing them for the summer, give them a good airing on a dry, sunny day.

- Rayon is very inelastic, which is why it often sags when left hanging up. Either store flat or stuff well with tissue paper and hang dresses from loops attached to the waistband instead of from the shoulders.

- Silk should be well padded with tissue paper, especially if the fabric is thin. Store silk knits and sheer silks flat. Cover all silk completely to prevent fading. White beeswax put in the container is said to keep white silk from yellowing.

- Bridal veils and hats and wedding gowns must be professionally prepared for storage (see Chapter 10).

- Small fur pieces can be stored at home, in a refrigerator or some other cold, dry spot.

- Keep clothes off the floor if flooding is at all possible, and keep whites in separate containers from colors.

- There are special containers for long-term storage. The easiest to use are zippered cloth, plain, or quilted hanging bags, or thoroughly clean and fresh-smelling old trunks and suitcases. Of course, the ideal is a fully cedar-lined closet or chest.

Why go to such trouble? You'll save more than enough in dry-cleaning costs and time spent in washing and ironing to make the trouble worthwhile.

CHAPTER SEVEN

Making A-Mends

The mending described in this chapter is the everyday kind, easily accomplished even if you're inexperienced. Just remember, the first time is always a learning experience. For bigger jobs find a pro or refer to a detailed sewing book.

WHAT YOU NEED

Keep everything in a large sewing basket or drawer *divided into compartments.* Otherwise everything's a jumble and you'll put off doing the job because you'd have to sort through the mess first.

Needles: An assortment of Nos. 5 through 10 will meet most needs (the higher the number, the shorter and finer the needle). You may also want fine blunts for mending knits, darners for darning, and basting and embroidery needles for doing fine, small stitches. You may also find a use for large-eyed embroidery needles—for instance, for mending sweaters with yarn.

Thread: Maintain a supply of thread colors and types keyed to your wardrobe, in medium (Size 50) and heavier weights. Mercerized 100 percent cotton is ideal for general sewing, as it is strong and elastic and won't shrink. A good sewing shop should have it. Skip those packaged thread selections in dimestores; they are low-grade. (For travel, make up your own selection of seven or eight colors of thread and wind them around a cardboard strip.)

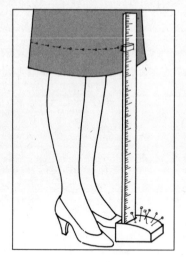

Cotton-wrapped polyester thread is best for knits and man-mades because it's stretchy. Use silk thread for fine work on silk and wool. (Only specialty suppliers will carry silk thread, of course.) It doesn't lint or leave a mark and is strong and elastic.

For heavy-duty repairs and for heavy buttons use glazed, waxed, or silicone-finished (labeled Boilfast) thread. It is sometimes called buttonhole twist, left or right twist, or heavy-duty thread.

Beeswax: Buy this in a container with slits to accommodate the thread. It is used to coat nonwaxed thread so it won't curl and will slip more easily through cottons and wools. *Don't use on silk, nylon, or polyester*, as it may stain them. Rubbing beeswax on zippers helps get them going.

Scissors: You need one or two pairs of stainless steel or hardened steel, including one with six-inch blades. Locate a scissor-sharpening service to keep them sharp—and keep them *sheathed.*

Measuring Tape and Marker: Sometimes flexible tape is useful, but for marking hems the standing hem marker is best. A yardstick will do, too.

Pins: For most purposes you need the regular and large-size steel dressmaker's pins, since they don't rust. To pin clothes out while they dry, as in blocking a knit, use the ones with T-shaped heads. A set of fine pins is a good idea if you work with silk.

A Pincushion: A good one is the standard firm red pumpkin shape, the larger the better. The little strawberry attached is a pin sharpener: just push the pin in and out several times to clean and sharpen it.

Various Fasteners: Have on hand a supply of safety pins in brass (small) and steel.

Hooks and eyes—the wide, flat type are for waistbands and the smaller silver and black ones for lightweight fabrics and low-strain areas—are useful. They are needed wherever a closure must stand up to pull. (Straight eyes are for when fabric overlaps; round eyes are for when two pieces of fabric butt up against each other.)

Snaps are used where there's overlap but no pull. Buy the sheets with assorted sizes in black and silver. For coats, use the big cloth-covered snaps.

Nylon (Velcro is the most familiar brand name) tape comes in various shapes and sizes. It's a good substitute for snaps, especially for children and the elderly, but the pieces must be sewn, not ironed, on.

Crochet Hooks: These are a boon when you need to even out snagged threads or pull them to the back of the fabric. Two or three in fairly small and slightly larger sizes should suffice.

Pill Scrapers: A little gadget like the D-Fuzz-It or even a single-blade safety razor will do for natural fibers, an electric shaver for synthetics. *Do not shave napped fabrics!*

Elastic: You will probably buy this only when you have a specific job in mind, since that will determine the width and length of elastic necessary. But do buy the firmly constructed webbing type that doesn't curl.

Thimble: It should fit the middle finger of your sewing hand.

Miscellaneous: In general you will need these items only when you have become an enthusiastic mender:
- An embroidery hoop in a 7-inch size is handy for holding fabric taut while doing mending, particularly darning.
- Seam sealer is a new product that seals raw (unfinished) seam allowances and will withstand a good deal of washing and dry cleaning. Try it as a substitute for binding, or closing, seam allowances.
- Fabric-glue sticks are handy as substitutes for basting, if you would rather not sew. The glue washes out later.
- Iron-on tape and patches come in various shapes, weights, and colors. Some are for washable clothes only, as dry cleaning dissolves the bond. Some are made to be dry cleaned as well.
- Waistband liner comes as either firm twill tape or, for dressy clothes, a heavy grosgrain ribbon. Buy the right length and color as needed.

STITCHES ━━━━━━━━━━━━

There are a number of stitches that you can use for repairs. The choice depends on the job. As a general guide use the chart on the following pages.

BACKSTITCH

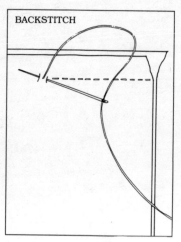

RUNNING STITCH

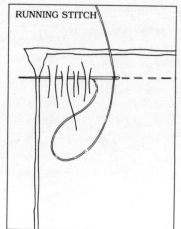

SLIPSTITCH

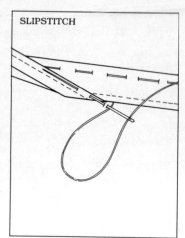

BAR TACK

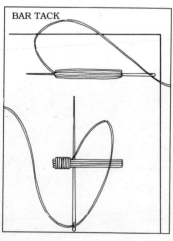

TOP STITCH

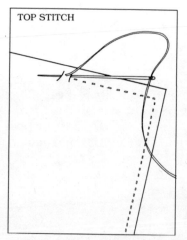

RUNNING STITCH FOR HEMMING

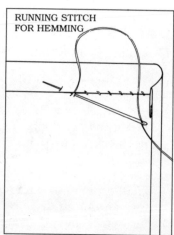

BLIND STITCH

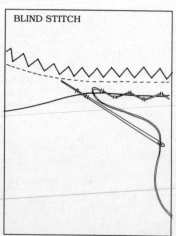

RUNNING HEM (WHIP STITCH)

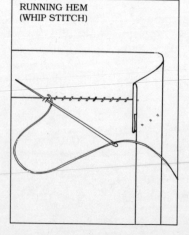

OVERCAST

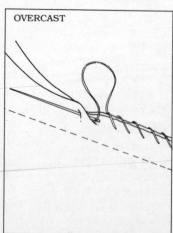

WHICH STITCH?

For Seams	For General Repairs	For Hems
Backstitch, for firm sewing	Backstitch	Running stitch, to sew down the edge of hem allowances
Running stitch, for quick repairs	Bar tack	
	Slipstitch	Overcast to bind edges
Slipstitch, for small repairs	Topstitch	
		Blindstitch
		Hemstitch
		Slipstitch

A serviceable stitch is about 1/8 inch long, except where noted in the directions. (*Basting* stitches—basic running stitch, but using longer stitches—can be 1/3 to 1/2 inch or longer.) You will avoid off-kilter mends and puckers if you first pin the pieces in place and then perhaps baste them. Work on a flat surface while positioning fabric.

SEWING TIPS —————————————

- Keep some needles threaded in the colors you commonly use ready in your pincushion. A 15-inch length is manageable.
- Cut thread *at an angle.* To thread a needle, dampen the thread and push the needle at the thread, not vice versa, or use a threading gadget.
- Instead of knotting thread, just make three or four small stitches one over the other both to get started and to finish. This is called tacking.
- Don't use a seam-ripper gadget; even expert sewers have accidentally ripped fabric with them.
- Use old spools to roll up ribbon—especially velvet—and tape. Secure the ends with a pin.
- When you work with stretchy fabrics like knits, be sure to make the stitches slightly loose so they give. When sewing a stretchy material to a flat, firm one, stretch the elastic side a little *as you go.* The stitches will then have the necessary give and the flat material will gather evenly.

The point to remember about repairs is that the sooner you get to them, the better. Loose buttons are easy to lose, rips and loose hems unravel quickly, and a missing fastener puts strain on fabric and seams.

The best way to get repairs done is to keep your mending and sewing supplies in a drawer close to your phone. It's surprising how many small jobs can be done while you're involved in conversation.

Forget about tackling complicated repairs. Mending welts—the material into which a pocket flap is set or the reinforcement at the edge—fly fronts, zippers, and hard-to-get-at seams are for skilled professionals.

As straightforward as our methods are, do read them over carefully before going to work. Check to see that you have necessary supplies readily available.

PREVENTIVE MEASURES ──────────

These small jobs are partly preventive maintenance, partly a way of compensating for the skimping on sewing that is a growing trend at all levels of manufacturing.

If you have examined clothes inside and out, as was suggested in Chapter 1, the things you have bought should have no major flaws. But there will be a number of small things to take care of when you get the clothes home:

- Clip off all loose threads, *except* button thread and buttonholes. *Never pull or bite thread,* because if there's chainstitching, it will pull out.
- Anchor buttons. If there is loose thread, pull on it just enough to give you several needle lengths, then thread and sew down several times, finishing with three stitches through the thread shank instead of a knot. If there's not enough loose thread, match the thread as best you can and, starting with several stitches in the fabric under the button, proceed as above. Reinforce snaps in the same way.
- Reinforce buttonholes by tacking down any loose threads.
- Reinforce stress points in small areas—the underarm seam, for example, or the point where the shoulder seam attaches to the neckpiece or collar—with a few stitches. Don't make these stitches tight if the fabric is a knit. If clothes will experience rough wear, it may be worth your time to reinforce larger areas like the crotch seam. Simply do a second row of stitches, using

a backstitch, over the existing seam. (If you're hard on pockets, double-stitch the bottom of the actual pocket and put a bar tack at the bottom of a side pocket, as shown).

- Another area that needs reinforcement is the top of a regular pleat or kick pleat. Topstitch a small rectangle, keeping the stitches small and even. Topstitch the top corners of patch pockets as shown.
- Zippers won't pull out as quickly if they are bartacked at the bottom. Be sure the tack goes through all layers of fabric, however.
- Check that zipper teeth come right up to the waistband. Toothless tape at the top is an invitation to the slide to slip off. If you get stuck with this situation try to sew the waistband down against the top tooth. If you can't do that, sew a nub of thread sticking out that will keep the slide from coming off.
- To keep elastic run through a fabric casing from twisting, tack it with several stitches at each seam. This is also a good idea for elastic binding on lingerie, since such binding has a way of coming loose if one stitch is broken.
- Loosely woven fabrics tend to pull apart at the seams. Rather than put extra weight on this fragile material by double stitching, you can—if the material isn't sheer and the tape won't make the area too stiff—reinforce with thin strips of iron-on tape, particularly at stress points.

For meticulous people who don't mind wielding needle and thread, here are three projects really worth the trouble:

1. Underarm shields (cotton are best) protect silk, wool, and rayon from perspiration. If the shields are tacked rather than sewn in (or even attached with snaps in several places), they are easier to remove for washing. These are available in sewing supply shops.

2. A waistband liner, or waiststay, is good inner support for skirts—especially pleated skirts and skirts of long dresses that don't already have reinforcement inside the waistband. It keeps the waistband from rolling, protects the outer fabric from perspiration, discourages drooping hemlines, and allows you to attach loops for hanging. The liner should be of firm tape or grosgrain ribbon a little narrower than the waistband. Grosgrain, which is softer, suits light fabrics.

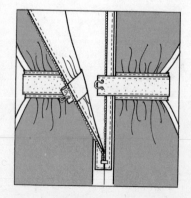

Make the liner 1 inch longer than the waist circumference. Tack it on where the outer material has seams or darts so the stitches won't show, and do the last two tacks 1 inch to either side of the zipper or closure. Next, fold the free ends over about ¼ inch, or enough to adjust the length to fit your waist snugly but comfortably. Sew these folds down. Attach an appropriate hook and eye to the ends with the open side of the hook facing toward the body. Optional: Sew loops of tape onto the waiststay of dresses you want to hang from the waist.

3. An undistinguished item can be made into something distinctive and stylish by substituting good-quality buttons for those provided by the manufacturer.

SMALL JOBS

Removing Pills: Pills are surface fibers that have rolled up into tiny balls. They not only spoil the look of clothes but pick up dirt easily.

They can be scraped off natural fibers and acrylics with a single-edged razor or a dimestore gadget for defuzzing. The firmer the fabric, the longer and more vigorous your strokes can be; just don't dig into the fabric. Work on a fairly firm nonslippery surface such as an ironing board.

Clip pills individually if the nap is long.

For strong, elastic fibers like nylon and polyester, sheering the pills off with an electric razor is easiest.

Lint deposits may come off with brushing or defuzzing. You can also try the plastic paddle with a velvet surface sold in most five-and-tens. It should be held at right angles to the grain of the material and catch slightly as you brush (turn it over if it doesn't). (Clean the paddle by wiping *along* the ribs with a damp terry towel so the lint gathers at the tip and can easily be picked off.)

Emergency De-Linter: For an emergency de-linter, use Scotch tape wrapped, sticky side out, around your hand. To prevent lint formation, keep lint givers (chenille, terry, soft cottons) away from lint grabbers (nylon, acrylic, durable press, polyester, corduroy, velvet, and other napped fabric).

Fixing Pulls in Knits and Wovens: For pulled yarns *not* runs (1), stretch and smooth the fabric up and down, then sideways to see if you can redistribute the loop. A crochet hook can often be used to even out the loop. If

What do you do when your child rips his best trousers or the puppy chews a hole in a treasured sweater? Find a reweaver/reknitter. They can handle small problems and some will also do patches on elbows and other large holes. *But* before committing yourself get at least two estimates and have a look at similar work they've done to see if it meets your expectations—these repairs can be expensive.

that doesn't work, use the hook to pull extra yarn to the back of the fabric (see illustration). It can be knotted against the back of the fabric, if there's enough yarn, or tacked down with a few small stitches.

Replacing Shoulder Pads: Many garments marked "Dry Clean Only" can be washed if the shoulder pads are removed. Unlined linen jackets are a good example. To replace them, fold each pad gently in half lengthwise and mark the center line by pinching it lightly. Set the pad to extend about ½ inch beyond the natural shoulderline—more for an exaggerated effect. Tack the pad to the armhole seam at three or four points. The center tack should be on the natural shoulderline seam. Or sew in snaps.

Replacing Hooks and Eyes: To position properly if there's an overlap, place the hook on the outside overlap so that the top of the hook meets the fabric edge. Close the opening and put a pin in to serve as the straight eye. Adjust it until you get the right placement. If there's no overlap, be sure the hook extends ¹⁄₁₆ inch beyond the edge and match it with a round eye with the curve extending ¹⁄₁₆ inch beyond the fabric edge. Pin until you get the right placement, then sew.

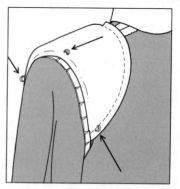

Replacing Snaps: Pin the *ball* side on the inside of the top (overlapping) fabric. Try the clothes on to be sure the fit is smooth and comfortable. Now rub the ball with chalk or carbon paper, depending on the shade of the fabric, and press it against the receptor side so it will leave a mark there. For a secure snap, sew through as many layers of fabric as possible without letting the stitches show. (Tape with snaps attached may be the easiest solution if you have to replace a series of snaps. You can buy it in various lengths at sewing supply shops.)

Attaching Nylon (Velcro) Tape: Pin the tape on and try the garment on for size. To sew, *either* slipstitch the upper strip through inner fabric and any interfacing, so the stitches don't show on the outside, *or* topstitch (on the fabric face) all the way through, use the stitching for decoration.

Replacing Buttons: When attaching a button be sure to make the thread shank (the length between button and fabric) long enough so that the button, when buttoned, sits neatly.

If you have to buy a new button or set of buttons, choose something comparable to the construction of the originals. For instance, coats and outerwear often have a

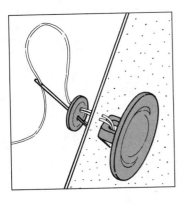

button with a metal loop underneath that can carry the weight of heavy fabric and wear. If you'd like to change the color of the button, fine, but look for one with a metal loop. If you must replace fabric buttons you can often steal material to cover them from the hem. Then you will need a kit, preferably one with *bone rings*, on which to make the new buttons.

If coat buttons keep coming off, anchor them by putting a small button on the back side of the fabric and sewing back and forth between the inner and outer button. With lighter fabrics, use a folded piece of ribbon binding on the back instead.

Sometimes positioning the buttons is a problem. To place one or two buttons, first pin the clothes closed. Button the remaining buttons. For horizontal buttons, push a pin or marking pen through the end of button-holes nearest the edge of the garment; for *vertical* buttonholes, mark ⅛ inch or so below the top of the hole. If you have to do an entire row of buttons, attach buttons one at a time from the top, checking the fit after each one.

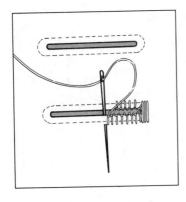

To sew, use a 15-to-18-inch length of suitable thread and take a few stitches on the top of the fabric where the button will sit to start. Thread the button on and sew, finishing with several stitches through the thread shank.

To Repair Buttonholes: If the buttonhole has completely unraveled, sew a line of small stitches all around the slit about ⅛ inch from the edge. Then do a button-hole stitch all around to bind the edges, covering the line of stitches you've just made. Finish with a bartack at each *blunt* end.

Replacing Drawstrings and Elastic in a Casing: Unpick any stitches securing the elastic (see p. 101), then open one seam so you can get at it. Pin the elastic on both sides of the opening so that it won't slip back into the casing, then cut it. Select a new drawstring or a fresh length of elastic with about 1½ inches for overlap. (Fold and sew down ¼ inch on either end of the elastic.) Now pin the new drawstring or elastic to one end of the old, unpin the old piece, and pull on it so that the new one slips into place. The new piece should be pinned, slightly stretched, to both edges of the casing so that *it* will not slip back in while you sew the overlap together. The sturdiest stitching is a square, as in the illustration. Once the elastic is sewn together, release it from the pins. Try

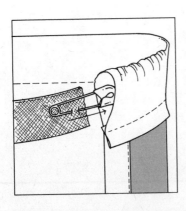

the clothes on to be sure the fit isn't too tight.

If the old drawstring or elastic is missing, pin a safety pin lengthwise—*not* crosswise—to one end of the new piece and use it to work the new string or elastic through the tunnel of fabric.

Finish by blindstitching the seam edges together again.

Resetting a Placket: Resetting a placket that has pulled out at the bottom or material that has pulled out of a waistband is really a fairly simple repair. Snip unbroken stitches so the placket is fully released. Trim frayed fabric. If the material needs a firm extension so that it will fit securely back into the seam, sew or iron on a suitable piece of tape. Insert the now firm and neat piece of fabric into the seam and pin so that no raw edges show. Adjust and repin so that everything is firmly in place. Resew using a slipstitch or, if the stitches are to show, a topstitch.

HEMMING, UP AND DOWN ———————

Keep in mind that you cannot let down hems in synthetic or durable-press fabrics because it's impossible to remove the old hemline mark. You can, however, make these garments *shorter*. (Pleats are very tricky to hem either up or down and must be taken to a professional.) The easiest materials to work with are plain cotton, linen, silk, and wool.

Unstitch the old hem, if any. Remove the old hemline by washing or dry cleaning.

To get hem-marks out of washables, see the entry for hemline stains on page 36. It may help to soak the clothes in lukewarm water with 2 tablespoons baking soda per 1 gallon water for an hour or so first. Rinse carefully. Press while still damp on the reverse.

Dry-cleanables should be cleaned *after* unpicking the

RESETTING A WAISTBAND

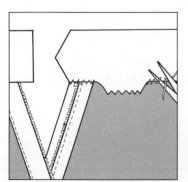
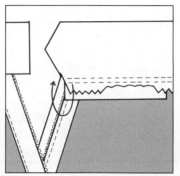
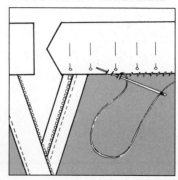

old hem. Mention specifically to the cleaner that you want him to get the old hem-mark out.

With clean wools, you can often steam the crease out yourself with the steam iron. Steam a few inches at a time well, then press on both sides, using a thin press-cloth to protect the front. Dampening the sections of hem with a little vinegar and water a few minutes before pressing them sometimes helps.

Hemming Tips

- For a perfect hem, fold the material up and pin it near the fold. Check. Repin if necessary. (This is where an assistant helps.) Next pin along the hem edge with the pins perpendicular to it. Make any adjustments such as darts to take in excess fabric now. Trouser hems should skim the arch of the shoe in front and come down about ⅜ inch longer in back so they graze the top of the shoe sole. Press the hem lightly, avoiding the pins. *Don't press anything until you are sure you have the right hemline!* If you don't want the hem to leave an impression on the face fabric, slip brown paper under the hem allowance while you are pressing it. Here are the different hems:
- Get a friend to help you mark the new hem. Put on shoes with heels of the same height as those you plan to wear with the clothes. You can use the original hem as a guide, but only if it was absolutely even.
- Trim off as much as possible, including extra seam allowances. (Of course leave enough hem allowance to be able to let the garment down later if you should want to.)
- With thick wools whose bulk makes hemming awkward, trim to about ½ inch. Then attach bias tape with a running stitch if the hem is circular or if the fabric is a knit, plain binding tape if the hem is straight.
- If you're letting a hem down and run out of hem allowance, sew ½-inch-wide binding tape (for dressy or light fabrics a lacy ribbon is attractive) to the hem edge with a hemstitch.
- With all raw edges, consider finishing them with an overcast stitch before hemming to make a more secure hem.

Straight Hems: Up to 2½ inches of hem is manageable, depending somewhat on the weight of the fabric. Shallower hems are easier to manage. You may want a deep hem, however, so that the weight of the extra material makes the skirt hang right or so that you have enough material to let the hem down later. Use a hemstitch, slipstitch, or blindstitch to attach.

Flared Hems: The fuller the garment is, the narrower the hem allowance must be to avoid tucks and bulk. A circular skirt, for example, would usually have no more than a ½-inch hem. Use your shears—pinking shears for delicate and easily raveled material—to trim. If raveling still seems likely, do a running stitch all around the hem edge about ¼ inch below the trimmed edge or sew on tape. If there is still bulk, pin in darts and sew them down with a slipstitch. Then hem with a hemstitch or slipstitch. NOTE: Wool can sometimes be steamed to shrink out a little extra fullness, but go easy, because you don't want to shrink the wool too much.

Tapered Hems: These are sometimes called funnel hems. Most are on pants. Trim the hem allowance to about 1 inch unless you might want to let the hem down later. Open the seams down to ¼ inch from the hem fold if the hem circumference is still too small. Tack seam stitches so they are secured. Now spread the seams apart so the hem lies flat. Pin in place. Hem with a hemstitch, slipstitch, or blindstitch.

Hems in Sheer and Lightweight Fabrics: Because these are delicate, the edge should be finished. One way is to trim the hem to about ½ inch, fold it over ¼ inch, and sew this fold with a running stitch. Then roll over another ¼ inch and hem with a blindstitch. Do this hem only if you have a perfectly even hemline and will never need to let it down. A simpler alternative is to pink the edges, do a running stitch just below the pinking, and then blindstitch the hem.

When finishing all hems, press gently. You do not want a hard edge, as it gets worn more quickly. Always press from the edge up, not sideways. Thick wools should be steamed rather than pressed, as should brocade and other heavyweight fabrics.

Specific Hemming Jobs

Putting a Hem in New Clothes: Be sure that all shrinkage has taken place, especially with cotton knits, corduroy, flannel, and denim. If you want to put in a temporary hem, allow for 3½ inches of shrinkage in these

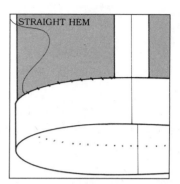

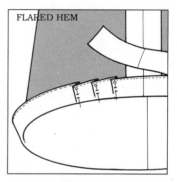

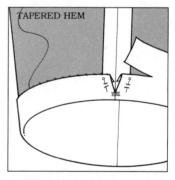

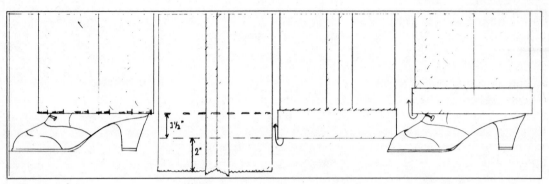

MAKING A CUFF

fabrics over the first four or five machine washings and dryings (if handwashed and air-dried they will shrink only minimally).

As an option, you can make a cuff until shrinkage is complete, and then let it down. Don't crease or iron the cuff down, or the crease mark will become permanent.

Making a Cuff: For a 1½-inch hem you need at least 3½ inches of extra material. With the pants on, mark the hemline length all around. Remove the pants, mark *1½ inches below this line,* so as to allow 2 inches of hem allowance. Then hem, using this second mark—the extra material makes the cuff when folded up, plus a hem. Check the cuff position. Tack at the two side seams with a few stitches to hold the cuff in place. When the pants need to be let down, simply cut the tacks and unfold the cuff.

Hemming Children's Clothes: Pants are done as for adults' clothes except for trousers with a lining attached to the hem. To shorten these, just fold the lining up the required amount and sew it in place. To let down, simply remove your stitching.

It's best to buy a jacket with some allowance left for letting sleeves down. Wool and cotton are easiest to deal with. When the child has outgrown the original length, unpick the stitches that attach the lining to the hem so you can extend the sleeve fabric. Press out the old cuff mark carefully, or have the jacket cleaned and pressed professionally. Then make a new hem and press it. If the lining is long enough, unfold it so it can be blindstitched to the let-out cuff. If not, hem it and then separately sew down the jacket cuff with a widely spaced hemstitch.

Mending Hems: After unpicking the old stitches, clean out the inside thoroughly. To unpick lockstitch, cut a stitch on one side of the line of stitches and pull gently but firmly till the piece breaks. Now cut a stitch on the other side and pull on that stitch till it breaks. Continue back and forth from one side of the material to the other as far as is needed. Reattach the hem with any of the standard stitches.

Reattaching the Hem of a Lining: If the hem of a lining was folded and attached to the shell fabric, copy the original placement and use a blindstitch to attach it. This stitching should be somewhat loose to allow the lining to float a bit.

BIGGER JOBS _____

Tears and rips are two distinct problems. A split seam is called a tear; a rip is a split in the fabric itself.

To repair tears, trim frayed edges of *clean* cloth. If the fabric is not too worn, pin it back to the original position. If the fabric around the tear is worn, you may be able to take a tuck or two so that you are working on firm material. If not, consider reinforcing on the back with iron-on tape (with a product appropriate for both washing and dry cleaning).

Once you have the right join, you can use a backstitch to do the repair. It's a good idea to make the repair with heavier thread or double thread, since the area clearly takes strain.

If there's a lining and you don't want to bother opening it up to reach the split *and* the split isn't in a very obvious place, you can usually repair it from the front with a very small slipstitch or running stitch. The slipstitch is better for knits and thicker materials.

With a rip, you can sometimes sew edges together as though they were a seam; if this is impossible, you can sometimes trim the broken yarns, iron on a patch underneath, and then sew back and forth over the split with a running stitch or dart. When repairing a rip where there is a hole, consider a reweaver. Otherwise you must decide whether to try a darn—best with holes of ½ inch or less—or to patch.

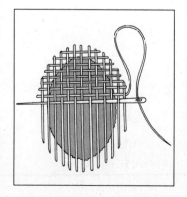

Darning: If you decide to do a darn, clip threads neatly but so they can be spread across the hole, if possible. Find the best match of yarn or thread that you can. Use an embroidery hoop to hold the fabric taut, face up. Sew as shown in the illustration, up and down yarns first, then over and under these lengthwise stitches from right

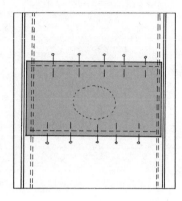

to left and back (reverse if you're left-handed). The darn must extend at least ¼ inch into firm fabric. Don't pull darn threads too tightly while you're sewing and smooth the darn between thumb and index finger occasionally so that it lies flat.

Patching: This method of patching is suited to largish holes and worn areas if you don't mind how it looks. It's practical for knees and elbows.

First, be sure cotton is preshrunk and that you have a patch big enough to fit; it's a good idea to save pieces of denim and other common fabrics you might want to use for patching. The piece must be ½ inch wider than the hole all around. Fold the edges of the patch under, pin or baste the patch in place, and press. Sew all around, using a topstitch, ⅛ inch from the edges, or a slipstitch around the edges, or both.

Cut-out Patching: Cut out the area *above and below* the hole and *from seam to seam*, including the half of the seam fabric attached to the damaged area. Pin the new fabric in place at top and bottom, then at the sides to make new seams. Baste in position, then press from the back. You will have two side seams and one top and one bottom seam. Backstitch these seams neatly. Remove the basting and press the seams open. Match the old stitching along the side seams on jeans and work pants with topstitch if necessary.

NOTE: A decorative alternative to cut-out patching and one that is particularly suited to children's clothes is the use of appliqués sewn over the hole. You can buy them or devise your own. For durability, first reinforce with an iron-on patch underneath.

Repairs need not be anxiety-producing. A little time, the basic supplies, and a bit of practice will add up to thoroughly presentable results.

A stitch in time, after all, saves . . .

The Compleat Man

Modern men are learning to take care of themselves and their clothes more and more efficiently, instead of leaving their wardrobe care in the hands of women. Many of the ideas in this chapter should appeal to the man who is learning to maintain his wardrobe and who is concerned about cutting down on costly dry cleaning and laundry care.

Men have some needs and problems different from those women face. Because they wear tailored clothes that cannot be handwashed, men must rely more heavily on dry cleaners than women do. On the other hand, they don't have to deal with sheer fabrics, hems cut on the bias, and other clothing problems that women face. Men's clothing is not as simple as it looks, however—either to buy or to maintain. Dry-cleanable items such as suits, coats, and ties need regular maintenance between cleanings to keep them looking good.

There is a short list of guidelines for buying a good suit, pants, shirts, and ties. For a more in-depth education, you should build a relationship with an experienced salesman at an established store.

SUITS AND COATS —————————

A tailored suit is the most expensive investment you're likely to make even if it isn't made to order, or custom-made. Aside from style, it's the construction that determines how a suit holds up.

Don't want to feel wild and woolly? Here's a quick pick-me-up for wool suits and coats: Mix a solution of
- **¼ teaspoon of ammonia**
- **1 cup of water**

Dip a sponge in, wring it out, and go over the fabric lightly, working *against* the nap. After rinsing the sponge in plain water, go over the clothes again, working *with* the nap for a smooth finish.

- You can expect ten or more years of wear from a 12-ounce or heavier weight wool.
- *Any* tailored suit *must* have some handwork in it to justify the term . . . and the price. Handsewing allows for "give" at places that take strain. You can get a rough idea of how much handwork was used in a suit by asking the salesman for the manufacturer's grading number. The scale runs from X for no handwork to 8 for a completely handmade suit. A 4 is standard for a good ready-made suit.
- Tailoring is the process of shaping flat pieces of fabric to the three-dimensional human body. A curved and slightly tapered sleeve, for example, fits the natural curve of the arm.
- Neither handwork nor tailoring can make up for a bad fit. *Don't be talked into a suit that needs any but the slightest adjustments of the collar, shoulders, or lapels.* A suit is a complicated, interrelated construction, and even fairly minor changes in one area involve changes in another . . . and another and another. Make sure that the collar sits snugly against the nape of the neck.
- On the matter of fused vs. separate interfacing: there is no doubt that traditional separate interfacing is better, but it's too expensive to use in all but the high-priced suits. Any costly item should have the traditional interfacing. It can be felt as a separate layer if you pull the two layers of a lapel apart. Fused interfacing is essentially glued to the outer fabric. It varies greatly in quality and should be treated carefully by your dry cleaner. After dry cleaning it may come unstuck in places, causing puckers—which a dry cleaner can *sometimes* remedy.
- If your weight fluctuates, go for an extra easy fit and choose a suit made of wool or another natural fiber, since letting-out marks show in man-mades. Ask for an extra lining of cotton in the crotch and at underarms, areas that must absorb a lot of strain.
- The lining, which can be full or three eighths, must of course fit neatly inside the suit. A three-eighths lining means a full lining in the front but only three eighths of one in the back—down to at least an inch below the armhole. The lining should be a firm weave, preferably in a heavy weight of rayon (rather than nylon or polyblend), that will give the outer fabric better support.

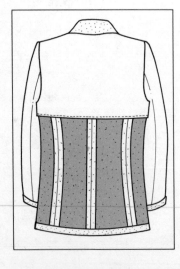

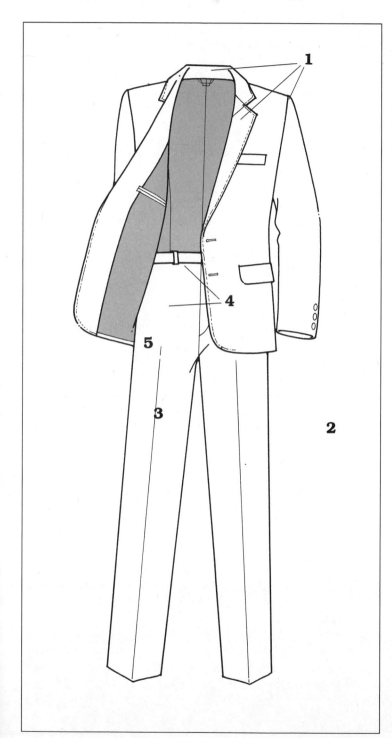

1: Check points for a good fit:
collar, shoulders, and lapels
2: Durable buttons
3: Extra cotton lining
at crotch
4: Reinforced stitching
at stress points
5: Waistband supported
by a firm liner

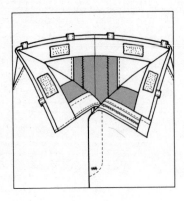

Pocket linings, however, should be of a tightly woven cotton or polycotton.

- Look for extra rows of stitching to reinforce places that take a lot of wear—pants pockets and the crotch seam.
- The undercollar (felting) should be a stretchy material, like wool felt, sewn in by hand.
- Buttons should be durable—bone, shell, or solid metal—with a thread shank long enough to rest neatly on top of the fabric when buttoned. Ask for one or two extra.
- Vents should have a generous overlap and hang neatly in place.
- Shirt grips inside the waistband keep shirts from slipping up. Although rows of elastic stitching work, tabs of napped leather (two in front, two in back) are better.
- "Self-healing" zippers are practical.

SHIRTS

- Dress shirts should be all cotton or a 60–40 cotton-poly blend.
- The best buys for knits are combed and/or lisle cotton. The yarns are stronger, more resilient, colorfast, and resistant to pilling and staining. They also iron up more easily in woven fabrics. Allow for one full size of shrinkage in the less expensive cotton knits—unless they're marked preshrunk. Return shirts that shrink more or, as happens occasionally, become a totally different shape after washing.
- Tailored shirts last longer if seams are overlapped and sewn down with two parallel rows of what is called single stitching.
- Buttonholes should be set in a separate placket attached to the shirt front.
- Knits need reinforcement at the bottom of plackets. Tape sewn into the shoulder seam adds further reinforcement. Knits should be very elastic, so look to see that ribbing springs back to shape when stretched.
- If you want long wear, *don't* try to squeeze yourself into the tapered European cut when you're really the fuller American cut.

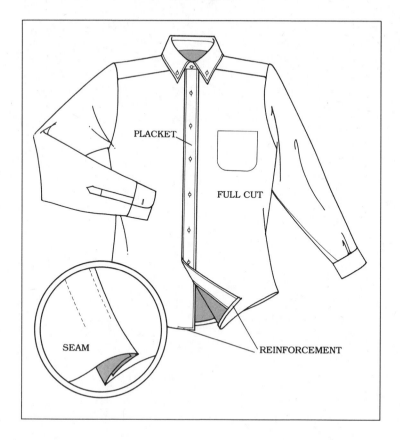

PLACKET

FULL CUT

SEAM

REINFORCEMENT

TROUSERS ━━━━━━━━

The most important thing, aside from a smooth fit, is sturdy construction at points of stress:

- The crotch should have an extra piece of cotton lining.
- The back seam should be reinforced with an extra row of stitches.
- The waistband should have a firm liner like Ban-Rol that doesn't snap and crackle when it's bent. This inner support takes the weight of the pants material and also absorbs pressure from the stomach.
- Belt loops should be secured *outside* on the top and *inside* the waist seam at the bottom.

- To withstand heavy wear, jeans and other work pants should have overlapped seams, metal plaques, or studs to protect points of wear and a short, heavy line of stitches called a bar tack both at the bottom of the zipper to hold all the layers of fabric together and at the bottom of slant pockets. Washable cottons need plenty of extra length to accommodate 4 to 5 inches of shrinkage. Wait at least 4 washings before shortening

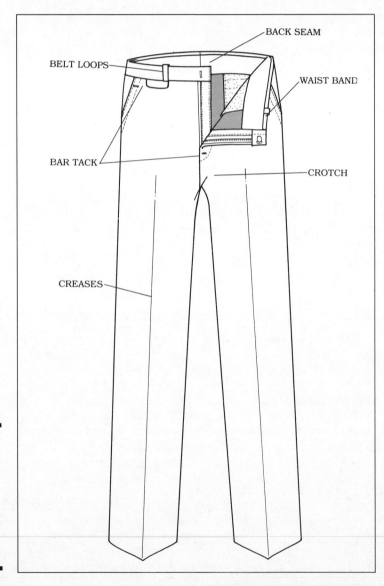

A man's skin exudes more body oils than a woman's does. To attack these oils in the wash, add a teaspoon of hard-surface liquid household cleaner to the regular wash.

them. (Pending shrinkage you can make a cuff. See p. 108.)

- Be sure creases—especially in man-mades where they are permanent—are correctly positioned and perfectly straight. If you put the inseam and outseam together, the creases should fall on the folds.

TIES

While there's a range of neckties from string to suede, the traditional silk or wool—occasionally cotton—four-in-hand is most worth looking over carefully, since it can cost quite a lot:

- Expensive ties should have a full-length *inter*lining that feels firm, not rubbery. The number of gold or silver stripes in the canvas interlining has nothing to do with quality. The lining can be full-length or partial, but it should go right to the tip and be handsewn in place.
- The folds in the back of the tie should be loosely slip-stitched together to make the tie lie flat. At either end there should be a horizontal bar of stitches tacking the folds together.
- Squeeze the fabric gently for a few seconds and release. It should smooth out neatly even if it's a thin fabric. Neither the tie nor the edges should be pressed flat.

MAINTENANCE

Since so much of men's cleaning is done by professionals, day-to-day care and maintenance are where the wearer can significantly affect his wardrobe.

What You Need

- A mild astringent (not perfumed) such as witch hazel.
- A natural-bristle clothes brush with bristles that bend fairly easily.
- A lint-removing gadget. The velvet-faced one with a plastic handle works best.
- A whisk broom for those who wear sturdy tweeds.
- Proper hangers for jackets, pants, and coats (see Chapter 6).

Follow the guidelines in previous chapters for storing, airing, cleaning, stain removal, and wrinkle releasing. Here are a few specialized tips:

Old hockey or baseball jerseys need brightening? If they're synthetic, polycotton, or synthetic blends, soak them, for *3 minutes*, in a solution of

- **1 tablespoon of *automatic* dishwasher detergent**
- **2 gallons of warm water**

Slosh one minute more and rinse out *thoroughly*. Caution: Wear rubber gloves.

To cut down on accumulations of grime inside hatbands, mop your brow with witch hazel or another mild astringent before putting on the hat.

- Brush and remove lint from suits and coats using a stroke that first goes against the nap—usually bottom to top—then smooths it down. The clothes brush is for soft fabrics, the whisk broom for tweeds. Work with the garment folded once lengthwise and laid flat on a bed or other nonslippery surface.
- Steaming wool and silk should get out most wrinkles, but if those annoying creases at the elbow remain, roll a towel to shape and leave it in the sleeve overnight.
- Take pullovers off carefully—don't elbow your way out. And take your glasses off first!
- For easy storage, consider one of those inexpensive wicker trunks, the bigger the better. They're a good place for sports clothes, underwear, and anything else that doesn't need careful folding. You may have to rummage, but it's all *there.*
- Dry cleaning is often hard on clothes. If you steam, air, and brush your suits after each wearing, you can usually get away with dry cleaning them only three or four times a season—once just before summer storage. Naturally, a suit that's worn several times a week will need cleaning more often.
- Sometimes clothes need only a professional *pressing.* (This will cost almost as much as a full cleaning because of the labor involved.) Ask specifically that the lining be pressed.
- If a suit is really out of shape, ask for a reblocking. This can only be done by a specialist.
- To keep ties cleaner longer, use an astringent to remove skin oils from chin and neck, and don't hold papers between your chin and your tie.
- Refresh ties occasionally by wiping over them *lightly* with a sponge dipped in club soda and wrung out.
- Give a wool or silk tie a lift by hanging it to steam with your suits. Afterwards roll it up neatly (beginning with the small end) for about 20 minutes, then unroll and hang on the tie rack.
- Make the knot *soft* and never drag the knot loose with your forefinger—a habit guaranteed to ruin the tie.
- Hang the tie up when you take it off instead of stuffing it in your pocket. (If you can't hang it, roll it up smoothly from the small end and put in a *large* pocket.)
- Ask to see a sample job before you have a tie cleaned.

Keep an enzyme presoak by the bathroom sink. Every few days make suds with a handful of presoak powder stirred up in a sinkful of water and toss in all your socks. Let sit five to ten minutes, rinse in three changes of water, and hang them on the towel rack. They won't shrink, will get clean and deodorized, and will be within easy reach when you need them.

Cleaning a tie is worth the expense only if the tie hasn't been flattened and looks like new.

Stains

Stains on washable clothes can be flushed with water if they aren't greasy.

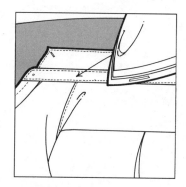

- For lipstick on a shirt collar, blot up as much as you can with an absorbent towel or blotting paper. *Don't rub*—you'll just spread it.
- For a soup stain on a silk tie, scrape up any surface matter gently. Blot for a minute or two, soaking up any liquid. If the stain is greasy, dust it with cornstarch or plain talcum, and when it gets gummy, scrape it off. Continue using absorbent powder as long as it seems to be soaking the stain up. Dust one more time and leave overnight. If powder stays dry, lift it off gently with a toothbrush, then give a final brushing with a soft brush.

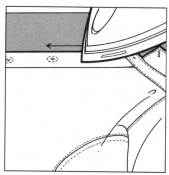

- Polyester ties can be handwashed (without wringing or twisting). Dab liquid household cleaner indicated for use on clothes on any spots ten minutes before washing. Silk ties must go to the dry cleaner unless cleaning fluid does the trick. As incredible as it may seem, the best way to remove a stain with cleaning fluid is to tamp and spread the fluid down the entire front of the tie. It won't remove the stain, but it will dissolve it and spread it out evenly. Be careful not to drag the tie out of shape as you work. Hang it up to air for an hour.

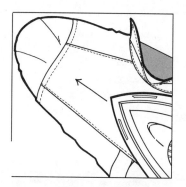

Ironing

With the price of sending shirts out, it can pay to know how to iron them:

- Buy a can of spray sizing—either starch or finish.
- Set the iron on the permanent-press or cotton setting—no steam.
- Unless the board is already padded well, cover it with a smoothly folded sheet.
- Take the dry shirt and, doing the small parts like the collar and cuffs one at a time, spray them evenly with sizing and iron.
- Use the tip of the iron as shown in the illustration. Do the inside first; then spray and do the outside. Use small strokes so as not to create those annoying hairline wrinkles and press from the edge toward the seam

of the collar and cuffs. (If the collar won't lie flat because it has loose material on the top side, it's best to stretch it face up over the tip of the ironing board while you press it.)

- Press both plackets from top to bottom, doing the bottom placket facing *down* and the button-hole placket facing *up*. *Press* over buttons instead of ironing so they won't snag on the iron.
- Now spray and do each seam carefully. *Press* the length of the seam and keep pressing until the material is just dry. This is important because it gives a shirt its basic outline.
- Iron the yoke, putting each shoulder over the square end of the board as shown.
- Smooth the sleeves out carefully or slip them over a sleeveboard. Iron the side with the button first, using the tip of the iron to get inside the gathers. Turn the sleeve over and finish the other side.
- It's easiest to do the flat parts by working from one front panel around to the other, always ironing up and down, with the warp threads of the fabric. As you finish one area, leave it in place on the board for a count of ten and fan it with your hand. This will set the press.
- Hang the shirt up for five minutes or so to air-dry.

You can devise your own system as long as you begin by getting the seams flat and straight. Courage: you'll be successful after a few trial runs. Plan to spend about ten minutes ironing each shirt.

Occasionally a suit gets a little rumpled but doesn't need dry-cleaning. Here's how to give it a touch-up.

- First, hang the suit up in a hot steam (closed) bathroom for about 20 minutes. If the knees are baggy, hang the pants up full-length with a pants hanger weighting down the free end.
- Set the iron for the appropriate fabric and on Steam.
- Fill the steam reservoir, using distilled water. Be sure the board is padded.
- To prevent shine, use a presscloth, a square piece of clean cotton, between the clothes and the iron.
- Iron each leg separately, working up and down, never side to side. Do the creases last, ending about two hand spans below the waist. Make sure the creases are properly positioned by matching the inseam and outseam and putting the creases on the folds. Traditional

Sweaty cottons can mildew. What to do? Put them in cool water with a few tablespoons of borax. Rinse, squeeze out, hang up. Voilà! Ready for the next run. (An alternative: Hang the clothes in an open window overnight.)

double-pleated trousers have the crease lined up with the pleat farthest from the fly.

- After steaming the jacket, press the *lining,* using a medium Steam setting. Press the rest of the inside. Finish by pressing along the edge with the tip of the iron. If you press the outside, be sure to use the presscloth.

Note that just as the rest of this book is applicable to *his* wardrobe, so this chapter is applicable to *hers.* After all, a suit is a suit is a suit.

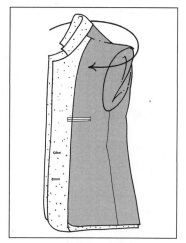

1.

After emptying the pockets, hold the jacket with one hand in each armhole and shake it out.

2.

Hold the jacket at the top of each armhole and flip the *body* of the jacket inside out. Shake it lightly to make sure it hangs straight, and adjust the lapels so that they overlap.

3.

Fold vertically so the armholes meet and the lapels are inside. Either drape over the back of a chair or fold once horizontally and set aside.

CHAPTER NINE

Leather Goods

Leather is expensive. To justify its price it must last a long time. Whether or not it does is partially up to you.

Cured and tanned calf, kid, alligator, snake, lizard, sheep, and occasionally pig and steer skins are commonly used leathers, and on the whole it's the finish—smooth surface, patent, oiled natural, or sueded—that determines care.

The most practical finish for regular wear is the familiar smooth, polished one, since its sealed surface resists dirt. Just be sure to renew the top finish regularly by polishing. Oiled natural finishes, though they scratch easily, are practical for workhorse articles like boots, luggage, and children's shoes because no top finish would survive really heavy use. Patent leather sheds dirt but can dry and crack relatively easily. Suede has some natural dirt and water resistance but needs regular care to stay presentable. Cleaning prevents dirt from working its way down into the skin. Very soft (or glove) leathers are fragile. (For washable leather gloves, see p. 134.)

When shopping for leather goods, established stores that do their own repairs are a good bet. Even so, assess each article carefully; its beauty may be only skin deep.

BUYING SHOES, HANDBAGS, AND BELTS ————————————————

- Durable leather is always top (full) grain, not a split skin. Lizard and alligator are up to ten times tougher than ordinary calf—which somewhat justifies their price.

- If you shop for shoes toward the end of the day, you'll get a more comfortable fit, since feet swell during the day. But watch out! Air conditioning can shrink feet deceptively.
- The best way to tell a good fit is if the shoes feel comfortable after you've walked around for a few minutes. Shoes that are too tight strain leather and seams; shoes that are too loose sag, crease, and become misshapen; both make a shoe wear out quickly.
- When checking the last, look at the fit from heel to ball of foot *and* from ball to toe—the vamp. Shoes with the right last for your particular foot will have a longer life and will be comfortable.
- Store finishes of shoes and bags *are not protective. Give the item a coat of proper polish when you get it home.* A good wax or cream polish is the only way to protect smooth, polished leathers from water, oil, spills, and color loss.

NEED NEW LACES? HERE'S WHAT TO BUY.

WORK/SPORTS SHOES		DRESS SHOES	
Pairs of Eyelets	Length of Laces (*inches*)	Pairs of Eyelets (*depends somewhat on width of shoe*)	Length of Laces (*inches*)
6	36	1	12
7	40	2	18
8	45	3	21
9	54	4	24
10	63	5	27
11	72	6	30
12	81	7	36
		8	40

Shoes

For a well-made shoe, look for:
- *leather* lining—allows moisture to evaporate and foot to breathe.
- leather sole for air-cooled comfort (rubber or synthetic, however, for hard wear).

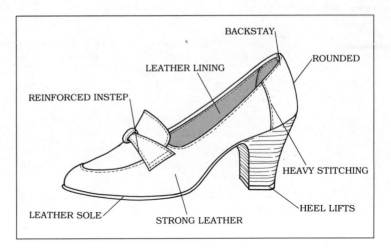

- reinforcement across the instep (remember the lace-up and the penny loafer?), where the arch of the foot puts a lot of pressure.
- heavy stitching where it holds the shoe together and isn't just decorative. Glued *and* sewn is a good combination.
- strong leather—if the shoes aren't just for dress wear.
- rubber/synthetic heel lifts on *solid* stacked wood or leather heels—for durability. (Be sure leather heel has a finish to seal it.)
- backstay—extra strength for shoes that get regular wear. In dress shoes this is a small tab at the top of the back seam.
- a counter—found inside the back lining. This stiffens the shoe as well as molding it more firmly to your foot.

If the shoe doesn't fit:
— Too tight? A good shoe-repair service can sometimes stretch shoes on a form or ease them by softening and stretching.
— Heel at the wrong angle so the sides bulge? Experts should be able to adjust the heel.
— Heel too short for you? The repairperson can usually put on one or two lifts (no more) to add height.

Handbags

When shopping for handbags, look for
- reinforcing rivets or stitching or a leather piece—needed to secure straps, for example.
- reinforcing leather or metal where stress or wear is likely—corners and bottom.
- metal decor and clasp of *solid* brass or steel, not cast metal. May be electroplated.
- sturdy, wipable lining—can be a good weight of vinyl, cloth, or leather.
- neat, sound stitching throughout.
- *finished* edges—no raw surfaces.

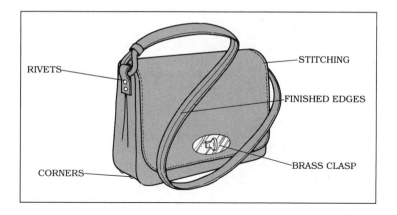

Belts

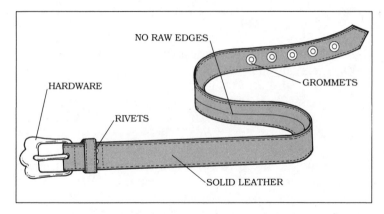

When shopping around for belts, look for
- one or more solid strips of leather—not a thin cover glued or even stitched to a backing.
- carefully sewn-on extra piece attaching buckle to belt. May be reinforced with rivets.
- no raw, unfinished edges.
- grommets (metal hole reinforcements), especially if the belt is to be cinched tight.
- solid hardware—as for handbags.

Care and maintenance are of particular importance for leather goods. The basic goals with *any* leather are
- to maintain the surface finish, if any, to protect the leather against dirt and spills.
- to keep the leather supple by using preservatives where possible and keeping it away from heat.

- to keep perspiration from weakening it.
- to maintain the shape.
- to have repairs made promptly to prevent further problems.

Obviously, the more you use something, the more often it will need care and cleaning. You can save yourself the trouble of full polishing and cleaning by practicing preventive maintenance.

LEATHER CARE

What You Need
- flannel for dusting shoes and bags before using them.
- soft, clean rags (old towels, diapers, or cotton cheese-cloth are ideal) for cleaning.
- more flannels for buffing.
- soft, fine-bristle brushes about 7 inches long for polishing—one for colors, another for neutrals.
- distilled white vinegar.
- colored and neutral shoe polish in tubes, jars, or cans—choose neutrals for bags and belts because you don't want color to rub off on clothes. Tube and jar polishes are usually lotions or creams and give a softer shine than the solid polishes in cans, which have a higher wax content. Men usually prefer the high shine of a wax polish. The best polish gives a hard, bright finish *only* when elbow grease is applied. Never use so-called self-shine polishes; they're alcohol-based and not only dry leather but seal the surface so it can't be nourished properly.
- leather cream or lotion that cleans and preserves or conditions.
- old toothbrush.
- rubber sponges.
- 00 sandpaper.
- clear dishwashing liquid.
- shoe and boot trees of wood or plastic.
- shoehorns.
- Optional: a suede brush, spray-on kitchen wax, weather- and stain-proofing spray (those without silicone are best for leather*), saddle soap, neat's-foot oil

*Silicone tends to yellow with age.

When you scrape a shoe or bag and a chunk of the leather surface peels away, you can glue the peel down with a glue that's made for porous materials. A little dab'll do it; then press down on the patch gently but firmly and *immediately* wipe off extra glue. Wait overnight before cleaning and polishing.

(or 100 percent mink oil) and white *cream* polish or, for buckskin, white powder polish sold for baby shoes.

Shoes

Each type of leather has specific needs. Although labels on cleaners, polishes, and oils are sometimes informative, you may have to experiment a bit to get the right combination for a particular leather. Always dust shoes before cleaning or polishing.

Here are some useful tips on general shoe care.

- Never wear shoes two days in a row. They need a day to air-dry and if possible another to recover their shape.
- Tree your shoes, stuff them with crumpled paper, or put them on a shoe rack. Never let shoes lie in a heap, where they scuff each other.
- Use a shoehorn and *untie laces* before taking shoes off.
- Travel with shoebags even if they're just old socks.
- When shoes are resoled, consider one of the new, extremely thin synthetic or rubber half soles if the shoes get hard wear, and have new *leather* insoles put in, both to fight odor and to strengthen the shoe. You can also put in a charcoal-containing odor-eater.
- Dust the insole with talcum if you aren't wearing socks or stockings.
- Give work boots, hiking boots, and other outdoor footwear a protective coating depending on the leather: first apply saddle soap; after the leather has dried somewhat, apply neat's-foot or mink oil for smooth leathers or a weatherproofing spray on sueded finishes. (Do *not* use a spray on very soft, napped glove leather.)

Smooth, Polished Leathers

- Smooth, polished leathers of calf, alligator, or lizard need applications of cleaning/preserving lotion several times a year, especially if they get wet or salt-stained, *before* polish is put on.
- If there are scuffs, wipe over the area with a soft cloth dipped in vinegar, doing an area no larger than about 6 inches by 6 inches. (Warming the vinegar helps.)
- Now use a *fresh* cloth to pick up any loosened dirt.
- Let the leather dry a few minutes, then fill in any scuff

Spit and polish. If you haven't had master-sergeant training, here's how to get a high shine:

After cleaning the shoe, rub it briskly with a soft cloth to warm the leather, then apply a high-wax polish and rub it in. Now flick on a few drops of water and polish *hard*. Repeat wherever you want a high shine.

Frequent cleaning and conditioning is necessary to keep cowboy boots supple and protect them properly. Be sure to air them *at least a day* after each wearing. (If you like, apply a desalter to prevent damage from perspiration—it can be bought in specialty boot stores—or a water repellent.) While working boots will be of heavy-duty leather that stands up to rough wear, reptile and other exotics like antelope and ostrich need applications of cream cleaner/conditioner after every third or fourth wearing. If you want your boots to be showpieces, use a heel and sole dressing on leather heels and soles.

marks with a dab of colored polish or a matching color of indelible felt-tip marker—the sooner you cover scuffs, the less damage there will be.

- In a few minutes apply a cream (for low shine) or wax (for a high shine). Neutral is fine unless color is needed where the leather is worn. Soft, dressy leathers need a low-oil, low-wax *cream*, while men's shoes normally benefit from a colored high-wax *paste*—in a jar or tin. Never put on more than a dab at a time and apply with a soft cloth. NOTE: Before applying a new polish all over the shoe, do a test area, as you may get an "allergic" reaction.
- Buff with a flannel.
- Finish after a minute or two with a brisk brushing—it will spread polish evenly as it brings up a shine.
- Electroplated metal trim can be shined with spray-on kitchen wax.
- Metallic-finish leather occasionally needs to be rubbed gently with a neutral cream polish.
- Patent leather and vinyl need special treatment. If there are marks, wipe over them with vinegar. Rub the shoe gently with a soft cloth, then polish with a spray-on kitchen wax, a window cleaner, or a commercial patent cleaner. *Don't* use sticky substances like Vaseline, which attract dust and show finger marks. *Imitation* patent leather made of nylon or other synthetics and plasticized cloth should simply be wiped with soapsuds and then dried and buffed with a soft cloth.

Suede

- Although a silicone weatherproofing spray may be suggested for suede objects, it actually gets in the way of cleaning once the leather is soiled. The *non*silicone type can be removed and is practical on suede boots and bags that will be exposed to the elements.
- If new suedes are linty, pat all over with a thick pad of terrycloth to pick up loose lint.
- For a general cleaning of any suede:
  1. Go over the article with a dry *rubber* sponge or an artgum eraser. Dampen the sponge slightly to work on bad stains.
  2. Use a suede brush *carefully* on gummy spots. If a bald spot appears, try rubbing lightly with 00 sandpaper to lift the nap.
  3. Brush over with a dry rubber sponge to lift the nap.

4. Use dishwashing liquid in water to whip up some suds and wipe over an area no larger than 6 inches by 6 inches with the dry suds that float on top of the water. Use slightly damp sponge or clean, soft cloth.

5. When the item is fairly dry, brush the nap up lightly with the rubber sponge.

6. An alternative to this thorough cleaning is simply to steam the article well—a boiling kettle will do—while lifting the nap with a toothbrush. When the article is dry, go over it lightly with a sponge dipped in water (and wrung out) to which a teaspoon of rubbing alcohol has been added.

7. Once it is dry, a suede garment can be steam ironed *on the reverse* on a low setting if it is wrinkled. Use a presscloth if the article isn't lined.

Natural, Oiled Leathers

These leathers characteristically have a matte finish in a dark or light tan. Stains are hard to remove, as the leather absorbs them even when it is well oiled.

- If you prefer a firmer feel, look for leather preservatives that specifically say they won't soften leather.
- Use saddle soap to clean, if you don't mind the fact that it darkens and softens leather. When the article is nearly dry, rub in a leather preservative or neat's-foot or 100% mink oils. Rub well with a soft cloth.

Handbags

If you want a favorite bag to travel with you for years to come,

- Protect it from scrapes by regular cream polishing with a neutral polish.
- Don't hang it by the strap, which should be folded neatly and put inside the bag.
- Prevent inside spills—put perfumes and other messy or loose objects in a waterproof pouch.
- Don't overstuff it.

Belts

To keep a belt in shape:

- Hang it up by the buckle so that it falls straight rather than curling it up in a drawer.
- Moisturize smooth leather belts with a leather preservative, either a lotion or cream. Rugged belts can be treated like work boots.

To keep the wet out of work boots and hiking boots: Melt about ½ cup of petroleum jelly and ½ cup of paraffin wax in a pan set over hot water. When warm, apply sparingly with the fingers to the boot. (Never leave near an open flame.)

- Don't buckle it too tight. The strain will show on the leather and take its toll on stitching.

STAINS

Leather is naturally somewhat water resistant, but it absorbs grease quickly. If you can't deal with a stain promptly the leather will swell and/or darken and the damage may be permanent. Sometimes a leather specialist can treat a stain, then recolor and refinish the area.

For a grease spot, blot firmly with an absorbent cloth for several minutes. Then clean as usual—on a smooth, polished leather, vinegar will sometimes do the trick.

For water and water-based damage, here's what to do:

- For regular polished leather, shake off surface material. *If the leather is clean,* wipe over while wet with a little castor oil, then wipe off any surface oil with a cloth. Stuff the article to shape it while it dries. Leave for 12 hours in a warm, dry spot—*not* near a heater— then use a preservative cleaner and rub with a clean cloth, then polish as usual. *If muddy,* clean up with a slightly damp sponge, then apply warm vinegar with a cloth. Let dry a while, then continue as above. Do the same for *salt* stains.
- For very soft polished leather, skip the castor oil step and stuff *lightly* so the leather doesn't stretch out of shape.
- For oil finishes, let any mud dry first, brush off, and then saddle-soap and apply oil as in ordinary cleaning.
- For suede, shake off surface water. Allow it to dry. Clothes should dry on a hanger; shoes should have a tree or paper stuffing. Lift off any dried mud with a toothbrush. Then restore the nap as described under general care.
- For patent leather, mop up moisture with a soft cloth. Let dry, then clean as usual.

REPAIRS

When it comes to shoes, the sooner repairs are done the better. Untended damage leads to related damage that can be difficult or expensive to fix. Word of mouth is probably the best way to find a good shoe-repair person.

Basic repairs include replacing half soles, the bottom heel lifts, and insoles. You can also have rubber or leather taps put on shoes to reinforce areas that get the most wear.

Repairs that require an expert include replacing a heel (it must be the same height and support the shoe at the same angle, but it can be a different shape), replacing a toe cap with a complementary colored leather or removing it for an open-toe effect, and having leather fully re-dressed. (Re-dressing removes the old finish, recolors and restores the leather, then replaces the finish.)

All repairs should be neatly done: no raw edges, leftover glue, or stains on the uppers.

When you need a handbag or belt repaired, find a specialist if you can. Not all leathers can be effectively repaired. Patent and metallic leathers are all but impossible to fix.

Basic jobs include reattaching and/or replacing handles and straps and replacing linings, zippers, and metal trim. You may want to ask for extra stitching and brass studs to secure straps or a belt buckle. Experts can also smooth leather, resew a badly deteriorated bag, and even reattach beads, but this is very expensive.

Before agreeing to a repair, be sure you've approved of the materials to be used as well as all parts of the job to be done.

Mildew can often be removed from smooth, patent, or grained leather with a small amount of vinegar. Wipe on with a cloth, then wipe over with a fresh cloth. Repeat until all the mildew is gone. Clean and wax. With unfinished smooth leather, scrub stains with saddle soap, then leave in the sun for a few hours.

STORAGE ────────────

- Before any leather is put away, it should be cleaned and, if called for, polished, then wrapped in cloth or paper to keep dust off.
- Stuff shoes with paper or fit on a tree to keep the shape. Stuff handbags with paper.
- Leather needs to breathe. Don't store leather articles in airtight containers.
- Leather can mildew. Be sure the storage area is reasonably dry.
- Don't use mothballs with leather.

CHAPTER TEN

From Down to Wedding Gowns

DOWN

Down is the fluffy undercoat of certain fowl. Although eider and goose down are reputed to be better than duck, good-quality duck in a well-made piece of clothing or comforter is perfectly serviceable. When shopping for a down-filled article:

- First establish the down vs. feather content. Feathers not only cost much less—so you should pay less—but also puncture the covering easily, don't last as long, exude oil that can stain the outer covering, and aren't as warm or as soft as down.
- To be really warm, down must be ample and sewn into numerous separate sections that provide an even cover.
- Top quality will have a shell of very high thread count (at least 220 per square inch) cotton or mostly cotton blend. It should have a water-repellent finish. If you do buy clothes with a nylon shell, be sure the fabric is a heavy weight.
- A separate lining will add enormously to the warmth of a down coat. The best construction employs a shell over the down, which is contained in an inner casing. (You can feel the separate layers of fabric.) You also want a fabric placket covering the zipper, a high, down-filled collar, and inner cuffs—or down-filled cuffs that turn back—to block cold air. Elastic sewn into the wrist edge and acrylic knit cuffs are the *least* durable designs.

When buying down for active wear, look for strong stitching at all points and a covering with some natural fiber content that will breathe, allowing moisture from the body to evaporate.

- Check seams for leakage. Put the item on a flat, firm surface and punch it a few times. If anything comes out, it's not properly down (or feather) proof. Look for even stitching, seam allowances that are sewn closed, and no gaps when you hold the seams up to the light.
- Washable items last longer and are easier to care for.

Down itself is *washable*, and dry cleaning is not good for it. But dry cleaning is called for if the item is unmanageably large or if the shell fabric won't wash well. If solvent smell remains after dry cleaning, ask for longer drying time, hang the item out to air yourself, or run about 20 minutes in the dryer, on a No Heat setting. Clean or wash at least twice yearly.

First remove stains individually—laundry bar soap is handy for ground-in dirt. If the item is too large for the washing machine, clean it in the bathtub. Use lukewarm water in the machine, a small amount of soap flakes, well-dissolved, and the Gentle/Knit cycle. Do colors separately. If the garment is sturdy, you can run an extra (gentle) spin to extract more water. If you handwash, use the ordinary handwashing method and rinse especially carefully.

Allow 1½ to 3 hours to dry by machine, at least 6 to 8 hours on the line. Use low heat in the dryer until the item is fairly dry, then add a clean pair of sneakers or a few tennis balls while it finishes drying. This fluffs the down. Then air the article outdoors on a dry breezy day, out of direct sun.

Do not overdry. It's better to remove the article when it is slightly damp and air dry it than to overdry. If line drying, shake and fluff several times. Never put it away damp; down can mildew.

When storing down articles, do not use airtight containers. Down needs to breathe. Don't crush. Store in a cool, dry place, taking extra precautions against mildew.

You can "downproof" an article somewhat by spraying it with a commercial water repellent like Scotchguard or Zepel.

Fiberfill is an inexpensive down substitute of polyester. Look for the continuous-fiber type. It is anchored to the shell so it won't shift when washed.

Wash as for down or as the label suggests. It's usually machine-washable at low temperatures. It dries quickly

Loops are provided for hanging most down clothes. Use them. Since down clothes are basically shapeless, hangers aren't needed.

and should be dried on a low or permanent press setting and removed promptly.

Do not confuse fiberfill with kapok. Kapok is a plant fiber used as a filling for mattresses, life preservers, and sleeping bags. It *cannot be washed.* Only a specialty dry cleaner should be asked to clean kapok-stuffed items.

GLOVES ——————————————————————

Cloth gloves can be handwashed and shaped, while drying, on a towel, but leather gloves are trickier to select and to care for.

When buying leather gloves, try them on to be sure the seams are sound. *Don't* pull on the tops—ease your hand in after folding the top down, then work the fingers in one by one. You have a good fit if you can comfortably clench your hand and if the button or other closing falls at the wrist-palm join.

You can dry clean sheepskin, suede, kid, glacé (very shiny) kid, and buckskin. Find a specialty cleaner if at all possible, not a regular cleaner who simply sends leather items out. (It's hard to get them to take responsibility if something goes wrong.) Suede and sheepskin are recolored in cleaning, but neither color nor softness should be dramatically different. The cleaner should tell you what to expect *beforehand.*

If you stain gloves, treat them with this method of home dry cleaning:

- Rub spots lightly with an artgum eraser if the leather is smooth. The old method of using chunks of stale white bread also still works! Have the gloves *on* while you do this.
- White kid can be rubbed with powdered starch or French (tailor's) chalk, using a piece of clean silk. Shake any loose powder off.
- Try removing oily stains by leaving them dusted with French chalk or cornstarch overnight.
- Re-color black kid with indelible marker, then rub in a few drops of olive oil.

You can wash gloves if they are unlined; are of pigskin, chamois, doeskin, or calf (with or without string inserts); and have no hair or pile. Unlined capeskin may be labeled washable. If not, dry clean.

- Try not to let dirt get embedded. Leather withstands careful washing but not a lot of rubbing.
- Put gloves of firm leathers like pigskin on your hand when you wash. Do each color separately. Leather dyes aren't fast.
- Use lukewarm soapsuds, rubbing spots lightly with a nailbrush. (To make the leather supple, add a drop or two of olive oil to the suds.) Roll gloves off your hands: *don't* pull on the fingers. Rinse and pat out flat. Roll in a towel, then blow in the fingers to shape them and pat out on a dry towel.
- When partly dry, flatten and put on glove forms, if you have them, or massage to get the stiffness out and stretch *gently* to shape as they dry.
- Ironing is optional. Smooth the gloves, use brown paper as a presscloth, and press with a medium iron.
- Pull to shape and smooth flat after each wearing. Wrap in tissue and keep in a box or drawer.

HATS ————————————————————

Hold on to your hats—they never really go out of style. Shapes that go out of fashion make a comeback after a while. Fur felt, straw, and even some cloth hats are easy to refurbish if they haven't been badly stained or mangled.

When shopping for a felt hat, look for fur felt, which is an animal fur, and more durable than sheep's wool. It can be pushed back to shape if squashed, and can also be reblocked more successfully than wool felt. Pay special attention to the leather band inside the hat. It determines a hat's size, keeps the hat on your head, and helps preserve the shape of the hat. Good hats have leather inner bands.

To make hats last a long time and keep their shape:

- Stuff the crown with tissue. Use hat stands if they suit the hat shape and material. Or put them in boxes or big glazed-paper bags nestled in a tissue-paper nest. (Hatboxes from specialty shops sometimes have supports inside so the crown isn't squashed.)
- Bridal hats and veils must be prepared for storage by a professional.

A topping idea! When you check your hat at a restaurant, don't let the attendant stack another one on top of yours. The dirt inside *theirs* will soil *yours*. This goes for your closet as well!

- Keep fur hats in a cold, dry place such as a cellar or basement refrigerator, or put them in cold storage. They need a professional cleaning every year.
- Brush fur felt and wool felt hats after each wearing with a soft, long-bristle brush.
- To refresh a fur-felt hat, steam lightly, holding the hat about 5 inches from the teakettle or other steam source, then brush the nap up lightly. Do the crown, then the brim. If the nap is wet, let it dry almost completely before brushing. Blocking gives a hat a "memory"; it should hold its shape for years unless it gets soaked or is kept in an overheated place.
- For wool felt use a short, medium-stiff brush. Steam very lightly, as these hats don't keep their shape well.
- A light vacuuming with the upholstery attachment an inch or two from the hat and on low suction will also remove dust and bring up the nap.
- Treat stains by blotting them. Let *non*-oily stains dry and rub lightly with a *dry* sponge to lift the nap. If this doesn't work, try brushing with a toothbrush moistened with mild soapsuds, then repeat with clear water. Sandpaper, used cautiously, is an emergency measure for old, dry stains, but it will remove some of the nap. Dust oily stains with an absorbent powder. Scrape off. Repeat several times, leaving overnight if necessary, then vacuum. Treat stains on wool felt as for fur felt, but use as little moisture as possible.
- Have fabric hats dry cleaned if they can't be hand-washed. Request careful shaping by the dry cleaner. NOTE: Cotton and polycotton rain hats can be water-proofed by the dry cleaner. But if you can wash, stuff to shape with towels while drying.
- Use an artgum eraser to get surface dirt off straw hats, but be careful not to bend the straws or they may break. Then wipe surface over with salt water or a solution of 1 cup of water and ½ tablespoon of ammonia, being sure the sponge is damp, not wet.
- You can sometimes touch up colors with indelible marker. Try white chalk on a white straw. Wiping over with a cloth dipped in a solution of half alcohol and half water also renews some colors, though sun inevitably fades straw.
- To soften straw and add gloss to a straw hat, wipe with a soft cloth moistened with glycerin.

Beware the jewelry jinx. Knits, from stockings to glamorous jersey evening gowns, snag easily on spiky jewelry. Leave the rocks at home and settle for something without prongs or sharp edges. If you can't resist those treacherous sparklers, put them on *after* the knit goes on, and take them off *before* you take it off.

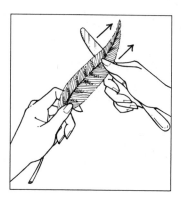

- A soft straw hat can be reshaped by stuffing it with damp paper and drying it with a hairdryer while you mold it to the shape you want. You can steam iron the brim and use spray starch to stiffen it. If this doesn't work, turn it over to a pro.
- To stiffen straw, brush on a light coat of clear shellac diluted with an equal amount of rubbing alcohol.
- When a professional renovates a hat, he or she should clean it, then reblock it and replace the lining, if any, and the inside band. Check these points before you settle on a price. You can ask for a new outer band, too.

Pay special attention to hat trimmings:

- Feathers are perishable. Treat gently. To refresh, steam lightly. To renew curl, warm near a heat source such as a hot iron, then draw a few fibers at a time between your thumb and the blunt edge of a warm, dry knife. Recurl, working from the quill out and from the tip of the feather down. Single plumes can be washed by dipping in warm soapsuds. Rinse in cool water to which bluing has been added if the feathers are white or black.
- Flowers should be kept dust-free with a medium-stiff makeup brush. Stiff flowers can be vacuumed. To reduce suction, hold your hand with the fingers splayed between the attachment and the flower. To revive stiff cloth flowers, hold petals *down* and steam lightly. To neaten frayed edges, trim with small, sharp scissors. (Coat edges with clear nail polish to keep them from fraying further.) To crisp and reshape cloth flowers, remove them from the hat and, using spray finish, carefully press each petal to shape with a warm iron. Ribbons can be removed, washed, and pressed or dry cleaned. Trim frayed ends as for flowers. Reattach by tacking to the hat with a few stitches.

KNITS ————————————————————

The last twenty years have seen a revolution in knitwear. The cheaper method of cutting pattern pieces from a bolt of knit cloth and then sewing them together has largely replaced full-fashioned construction in which each piece of a pattern is knit to shape before sewing.

Hand knits, however, are still knit and then sewn together. There is also a hybrid called a hand-framed knit, knit piece by piece on a machine. Such garments should perform like knit-and-sewn clothes. Be vigilant when shopping for knits. When well made, they last for years.

- Consider the basic construction, checking for well-aligned pieces and well-matched patterns.
- Check for good elasticity especially at ribbing. Knits that stretch out of shape easily or wrinkle are a bad buy.
- See that seams have properly elastic stitching by stretching and releasing. Seams should be flat, *not* puckered.
- Make sure there is reinforcement at points of stress. Cloth tape sandwiched in the shoulder seam is a good idea, as is a cover stitch on the collar, hem, and edge of sleeves. A cloth tab and extra stitching at the four-way underarm join is something you may have to do yourself.
- Check for extra yarn for mending—and extra buttons, perhaps—and careful detailing if you're being charged a lot.

Most knits are *washable.* They're more practical that way, especially since perspiration isn't removed in dry cleaning. Exceptions to laundering are novelty knits, natural-fiber chenille and bouclé, and anything with non-colorfast trim. Those old felt letter-sweaters must be dry cleaned, for example.

When in doubt about the washability of an item, do the test on page 16. Handwash those that pass the test. Even though labeled "Machine Wash," acrylics, nylon, and blends will pill much less if handwashed.

Although most knits should be dried flat—or on a well-padded rack—to keep their shape, interlock warp knits and double knits are firm enough to hang up. Acrylic hand-knitting yarns (Sayelle, Wintuk, etc.) need a brief machine drying to regain their shape.

Properly made knits shouldn't need ironing. Besides, the stretchiness of knits makes it easy to iron in creases. If you have to iron, pad the board well and steam *press* lightly, face down. Shake out and let air dry a few minutes before folding.

To hang or not to hang? Your cue is how stretchy the material is. The looser, softer, and finer the yarns, the more likely they are to stretch. Store these flat, folded as

Incredible shrinking wool knits? If badly shrunk, give up. If only slightly shrunk, and if you haven't been able to reblock them, take to be reblocked by a good dry cleaner. Most success: jersey knits.

few times as possible or rolled up smoothly. Try not to stack items nor to jam them too tightly into the drawer.

Firmer, heavier weights can be hung up when in regular use. Fold lengthwise, perhaps with tissue in the fold, and drape over a hanger bar.

For the long term, layer all knits with tissue and store flat or rolled in drawers or on shelves.

LACE

There are three kinds of lace: needle or bobbin, the true handmade laces, loom-made laces, and machine-made laces. Only handmade linen and silk lace is of real value. The less valuable loomed lace was made on pusher looms as long ago as 1825.

Fine handmade lace is a thing of the past—almost all of it was made before the end of the nineteenth century. What we have now is all we will ever have; it is rare and extremely valuable and should be washed (lace cannot be dry cleaned!) only by a well-recommended expert.

- The first and most vital thing to know about old lace is whether it is made of silk, linen, or cotton.
- *Handwashing* is always called for. An expert should do silk, anything valuable, and modern loomed laces like rosepoint and duchesse, since they cost upwards of $175 a yard.
- If you have lace of purely sentimental value and you decide to wash it yourself, here is the proper procedure:
  1. Unpick the stitching holding the lace to the fabric— unless you're dealing with trim that can be washed and ironed in the same way as the fabric it is attached to.
  2. Flatten the lace on a large piece of fresh stiff paper or muslin that you have anchored to a firm surface such as the ironing board. Now mark the dimensions by using pins to prick holes around the edges if you can't trace the outline with a hard, sharp pencil without marking the lace. The purpose of this is to return the lace to its *exact* original dimensions. Exception: Baste soft or very delicate lacy patterns to a piece of muslin before washing. Iron while still attached to this backing.
  3. If the lace is only lightly soiled, you can simply soak until the yarns are thoroughly pliable—use 1 table-

If a knit says "Block to Dry" or it's a soft handwashable wool, before washing it lay it out on brown paper and draw an outline of it. This will be your guide to reshaping it after washing. Wash by laying flat in the bathtub and squeezing suds through gently with a sponge. Drain the tub without moving the knit, run in enough clear water to float slightly, then drain the tub and press out water. Repeat until water runs clear. Roll between two towels, then pat out gently as close to the outline you've drawn as possible. Bunch somewhat to shape. Repeat bunching several times during drying.

spoon of baking soda in the water—then squeeze the piece gently in thick, warm soapsuds. *Never rub lace.* Rinse carefully in several changes of water, preferably distilled water.

- To dry, smooth the lace piece, then pin about every half inch—in the openings, not through the yarns—on the marked paper or cloth. Sturdy lace can be stretched gently to shape while winding it around a straight-sided bottle. Pin the ends to hold it firmly while drying.

- Lace is often tired-looking. Put it in lukewarm soapsuds—about 2 tablespoons of soap flakes or 1 tablespoon of liquid soap (castile is a good choice, or one of the textile soaps listed in the note on p. 152.) to each quart of water, and soften as necessary with 1 tablespoon of borax. Soak a few hours, rinse, and repeat if necessary.

- Brittle, discolored cotton and linen lace can be boiled in plain soapsuds for 5 to 10 minutes. This may remove mildew and/or oxidation stains, too.

  NOTE: Victorians thought white lace was gaudy and used tea and coffee, among other things, to make it ecru or pale brown. Use a mild bleach solution on such lace, but only as a last resort.

- Black lace can be brightened by dipping it in a solution of 3 parts water to 1 part white vinegar. Squeeze for a few minutes, then rinse.

- Avoid ironing if possible. If necessary, use a dry iron and a thin presscloth over damp lace. Thicker lace will need more padding underneath. Be very careful not to drag the lace out of shape with the tip of the iron. If you want a stiffer result, do the last rinse in rice cooking water *or* dampen the presscloth, then spray it with fabric finish or starch and press with this sized side facing the lace. Leave the lace in position to dry completely.

- To reattach lace, sew it on with small, even stitches using cotton thread. Linen thread is better, but is no longer available. Sew *between* the yarns, not through them.

Store all lace so as to avoid strain on the fibers and on the seam between the lace and the fabric if it's attached to clothes. Pieces of lace should be washed and aired on a dry sunny day once or twice a year. Don't leave them in direct sun.

- Contemporary lace (trim) is usually nylon or polycotton. If you have a choice, buy cotton lace, as it washes better and can be starched. Nylon picks up dye and soil easily and is especially incompatible with clothes that have to be dry cleaned or that aren't washed after each wearing, such as a wool sweater.
- Avoid lace completely bonded to another fabric; it won't wash or dry clean well.
- Check that the fit does not place strain on the stitching attaching lace inserts to the rest of the garment, as it will pull away easily.

LINGERIE, SOCKS, AND SWIMSUITS

The use of similar fibers links these wardrobe components. Lingerie and hose are predominantly cotton or nylon or both—with elastic—while swimsuits are usually nylon-spandex with perhaps some cotton content.
- Careful construction, not price, determines the value of these clothes, especially lingerie. Sometimes your best bet is a reliable manufacturer, whether it's down-to-earth Carter's or top of the line Eve Stillman.
- It simplifies care a lot to buy only one kind of lingerie— cotton or nylon. If you do own both, try not to throw the nylon stuff into the washing machine; it deteriorates rapidly.
- Buying several pairs of identical socks saves time, money, and energy, as it postpones the day when you end up with one unmatched sock.
- Elastic that has been anchored to the seams with bar tacks or even small pieces of fabric sewn over stress points makes for more durable underwear. Check out how elastic is attached, and be sure it feels stretchy but *firm.*
- Check that no stitches are broken by pulling gently in different directions and by holding the article up to the light. The stitching where lace and plain fabric are joined *must be* sound. Chainstitch, which unravels instantly, is also far too common. Look for lockstitch.
- As for swimsuits with spandex, look for a smooth but not too tight fit. Spandex under strain deteriorates rapidly, showing as puckering or as loops popping through the face of the fabric.

- Use only cleaning agents compatible with the most delicate fiber you're dealing with. Rub or use a soft brush when called for if the fabric won't snag or pill. *Handwashing* is invariably best for all these items. Always hang to dry if at all possible. Rolling in a towel for a minute speeds drying.
- If you presoak, always rinse out well, then wash in fresh suds.
- When badly soiled or too delicate to rub, presoak lingerie in salt water or an enzyme presoak solution.
- Nylon and nylon-blend lingerie and hose respond well to 2 tablespoons of ammonia dissolved in a sinkful of soapy water. Use cool or warm water. If you must machine wash, use the Gentle setting . . . and put in a zippered mesh bag if you want to prevent snags.
- Nylon-spandex swimsuits should simply be rinsed, right after use, in cool water and hung up to dry—not in direct sun. If *very* dirty use a mild detergent and lukewarm water to wash. To rid a swimsuit of suntan oil spots, use a grease solvent.
- Cotton can withstand warm or hot water, regular detergents, and even bleach, but the elastic will undoubtedly deteriorate quickly under these conditions, so beware.
- If you do put lingerie or hose in the dryer, run on low or permanent press *just long enough to dry the main fabric.* Remove while the elastic is still damp.
- Don't iron nylon-spandex. Most 100 percent nylon will not need ironing, and nylon tricot is a pain to iron.
- Resist the temptation to put any of these items away without careful cleaning.
- If swimsuits survive a season, give them added life by soaking in warm water with a tablespoon of vinegar added, then wash as usual. Stuff bras with tissue to shape them.
- Silk will yellow in time no matter what, but it helps to keep it in a cloth bag, rolled lightly in tissue paper.

RAINWEAR ━━━━━━━━━━━━━━━━━

One of the most important things to understand about rainwear is the labels: *water repellent* or *resistant* mean that water drops will bead up and roll off the fabric until the coating that protects the fabric wears off. These fabrics also breathe so you don't swelter in them. *Water-proof* means the article is guaranteed not to absorb water through the fabric or seams. Slickers and foul-weather gear should be waterproof. Unfortunately that means they're also *air*proof, so you do swelter except in very cold temperatures.

Cotton is the basic fiber for most rainwear. Silk, 100 percent nylon, and polyester are also available.

Some polyester content will make cotton more durable.

- Poplin and canvas weaves—in trenchcoats, for instance—have always been popular, since they are so tightly woven that the weave repels water to a degree.
- Silk is washable, if unlined, and travels well.
- Two-ply rather than single-spun yarns in any fiber are more durable, too, though that information isn't always available.
- The repellent finish should be of the fluorocarbon type (Zepel and Scotchguard, for example), since they are also oil repellent. Silicone finishes are oil *absorbent*.
- At least as important as the shell is the *lining*. Be sure it is preshrunk if you plan to wash a cotton jacket or coat. Ask if the lining has a water-repellent finish. It may add to the cost, but without this finish, the lining tends to attract water *through* the shell.
- A smooth lining slips more easily over such things as wool suits.
- A floating yoke on a trenchcoat gives you *two* outer water-repellent layers instead of one.
- Generally wash each item as the label specifies. Water repellency will last longer in handwashing than in dry cleaning, but both methods of cleaning are possible with cotton and silk if the garments involved aren't lined or are lined with *one layer* of cotton or silk.
- Slickers and other rubberized items can simply be wiped off with a soapy sponge. Gummy dirt should come off by rubbing gently with scouring powder.
- Pretreat spots before washing. This usually requires some patience, a nailbrush, laundry bar soap, and perhaps a stronger oily-spot remover, because few people wash rainwear regularly.
- Rinse very carefully to be sure there's no soap or dirt left to make the repellent finish less effective.
- With machine-washables, removing the item before the final spin will cut down on wrinkles.

- Take time to straighten seams and smooth the fabric while drying.
- Press silk, cotton, and polycotton while damp. You may be able to find a cleaner to do the pressing after you wash. It's expensive but will give a much smoother finish and a crisp shape. A trenchcoat or cotton poplin should be pressed to a crisp, smooth finish—no shine or impressions around pockets or buttons. The lining should also be pressed. All this involves hand pressing, hence expense.
- Resist the temptation to put the item away dirty.
- If you have the coat dry cleaned, renew the repellent finish about every third cleaning. You'll know it's time when even a light rain soaks right in.

TRIMMINGS

Belts
- Self-belts without backing or trim should be washed or dry cleaned *with the clothes they belong to.* Use a nylon mesh bag to guard against tangling in the washing machine.
- A belt with stiff backing must be drycleaned, although the vinyl and glue often used don't hold up well.

Embroidery
- When buying embroidery, try to find out if it's colorfast. Some is not and can ruin your clothes. Silk and cotton mustn't be washed unless you're sure they *are* colorfast. When washing, use lather skimmed from mild soapsuds rather than submerging the item. *And don't rub*—embroidery has numerous "floating" yarns that can easily be disarranged. Rinse quickly in lukewarm water to which a touch of vinegar has been added if you want to brighten the color. Pin out flat on dry towels to dry, and *don't iron. Press* face down on a very well-padded board.

Ribbon
- When buying satin ribbon and ribbon binding, look for double-face (identical on both sides).
- Dry clean taffeta and moiré silk ribbon.
- Before washing, test cotton, silk, rayon, and acetate ribbon for colorfastness, then handwash gently—no

rubbing. If shrinkage or bleeding cause problems with ribbon binding, and label instructions have been followed, you should return the item.

- Use a dab of clear nail polish to keep ends from fraying.
- Iron ribbons and bindings as the fiber and fabric suggest, *or* smooth and stretch flat on a formica, stainless steel, or glass surface until dry; ironing may not be needed.

Sequins, Paillettes, Beads, and Rhinestones

- When buying sequins, paillettes, beads, and rhinestones check that no pieces are missing and that each one is secured to the backing. Plastic sequins and paillettes (small sequins) are particularly fragile and often lose their color in dry cleaning. Ask for assurances that they will stand up to dry cleaning when you shop. Ditto for plastic beads. Look for rhinestones set into prongs rather than glued on.
- Most beaded articles must be dry cleaned because they are on dressy clothes, but things like sweaters can be handwashed if the sweater is washable and the detailing is firmly attached. It is safer to have elaborate designs handled by a cleaner. Rhinestones should also be handled by the dry cleaner. Except for touch-ups these clothes should be turned over to a skilled pro for pressing. If you do press it yourself, check that the backing fabric irons easily. Put face down on a very well-padded board and be sure the design is lying perfectly flat. Sequins and paillettes should all be facing the same way. Press gently. You can use a low steam setting if the backing fabric can be steamed. Some can't. Chiffon, for example, tends to shrivel in contact with steam.

WEDDING GOWNS ————————————

Old or new, no matter what the material, your main concern is proper cleaning, pressing, and *packing* between uses. Some fabrics store well; others do not. Discuss this with the salesperson if you plan to keep the dress as an heirloom.

- Also, if you buy a gown to hand down, ask that the lining be sewn separately to each piece of pattern or that it be detachable so that later alterations can be made easily. The best material for an heirloom gown is silk—satin, faille, peau de soie—or brocade. Cotton is also a good choice.

- When wearing an old gown, treat as suggested in Chapter 11, "Vintage Wear." You would protect it from *inside*, for example, by wearing the kind of underpinnings current at the time the gown was originally worn—a waist cinch with a tight-waisted dress, perhaps.

- Put clean sheets down on the floor to protect floor-length gowns.

- Hang up well stuffed with tissue where necessary and supported at the waist rather than the shoulders. Pleat a train several times, then loop up and pin to a padded hanger.

- *At the wedding* leave spills for professional attention later. Just blot them carefully, and dust oily stains with cornstarch.

- *After the wedding* take the gown to a specialist, whether it is new or old. The hand cleaning may be expensive and professional packing adds to the cost, but they are the only way to ensure that the dress survives years of storage well. The specialist cleaner has the know-how and the chemicals to get out most stains, and his or her trained staff will do repairs and proper hand pressing *inside and out*.

  NOTE: If the specialist does the packing, he or she should give you a guarantee about the condition of the gown provided you don't break the seal on the storage box and it is kept in a cool, dry place.

- If you pack the dress yourself, after a professional cleaning,
  — use a large, oblong acid-free cardboard box.*
  — Line the box well with tissue.
  — Spread the dress out and make a last check for stains, then stuff the sleeves with rolls of tissue. Fold the dress with plenty of tissue so that the bodice comes out on top with the sleeves extended. Cut a piece of white cardboard into a form to fit inside the bodice without stretching it. Make six or seven puffs of tissue about 6 inches long and roll smooth tissue around them. Use these "bolsters" to fill out the bodice well, with the cardboard form in the middle. (It will show above the sides of the box.)

*See sources, p. 93

— Tuck the sleeves down along the sides even if they are compressed a little. Finally, put lots of flat tissue on top and close the box, taping it shut. No mothballs are needed if the gown has been dry cleaned.

Do go through this process even if you might use the gown as a party dress. The gown will age badly if you just leave it hanging in the closet.

NOTE: Formal dresses needn't be boxed, though silk jersey and other draped fabrics should be folded and kept on a shelf or in a drawer. Stuff with tissue and hang from the waist with the bodice on a separate hanger. Cover with a sheet or get a cloth bag long enough so that the dress hangs freely.

CHAPTER ELEVEN

Vintage Wear

"Vintage clothes" is a term used to distinguish wearable period clothes from those antiques that should be preserved intact *instead* of being worn. These vintage garments require special attention in every aspect of clothes care.

BUYING ANTIQUE CLOTHES

The big question is, "How do you know a good buy?"

- Find out as much as you can about the article. If the seller can't tell you, turn to specialists in clothing restoration or a local museum with an interest in textiles or clothes.
- Check for stains and for signs of wear and strain along seams and fabric. Quality in materials and workmanship as well as overall condition should be considered.
- Pull silk gently side to side to be sure it hasn't reached the shred stage. Look for lighter areas where perspiration has made dyes migrate, since this is something that restorers can do little about.
- It is important to know not only the fiber used but also the *fabric*, since both of these determine proper care. On the whole, you will be dealing with natural fibers, since synthetics came into the picture only recently and often haven't survived well. The most important distinction to make is between the plant-based fibers, which are washable in the normal way, such as cotton,

linen, ramie (rare), rayon, and acetate and the protein-based ones such as silk, wool, and animal hair, like cashmere, which often can be washed but only in cool water with mild soap or detergent. The plant-based fibers also respond well to restoration, while protein-based fibers do not, once they have aged.

- In no case do you want to buy anything that needs more than minor repairs; the effort and expense will not match the reward.
- If you buy from a dealer rather than at auction you should get something that has already been put in good shape. It's the dealer's business to know vintage clothes; he should tell you about special care problems and, if necessary, give you the name of a professional to clean the garment.
- Don't scorn bargain-priced secondhand clothes! There's some value in period findings such as mother-of-pearl buttons and other interesting clasps and trim. These are getting harder and harder to come by and can be removed and used to advantage on other clothes.

CARE AND MAINTENANCE ——————

With few exceptions, about a dozen wearings is the most you can expect from vintage clothes. The strain on a beaded dress of the 1920s or a thirties slipper satin gown is considerable. Modern bodies are quite different from those of the past, and so is our way of life.

Therefore, when it comes to wearing:

- Consider having a lining added if there is none. Wear absorbent cotton underwear and dress shields. Also try to find out what the corseting of the period was and wear some sort of equivalent so that you minimize strain on the material. Women wore waist cinches in the fifties, for example, and they can still be found.
- Sew a grosgrain ribbon or twill waiststay into the waistband of skirts and dresses as described on page 101 both to take strain off the waistband and to enable you to hang the dress from the waist instead of the shoulders.
- Resist the temptation to wear the clothes for other than special occasions or for more than four to five hours at a time. And play it cool—don't expect "antiques" to stand up to disco dancing.

- After each wearing, lay the item out or hang it up on properly shaped hangers to air out. Examine carefully and spot clean or wash as soon as possible if it's needed.
- One of the worst things for old fibers is perspiration. If you can't launder right away, flush perspiration out with some mild suds, rinse with clear water, and let dry. Once clean, you can iron while the garment is slightly damp if the fabric calls for it.

Stains: Since old fibers are delicate, gentle stain-removal methods are called for. Having determined that the fiber and fabric are washable by using the information available in the fiber and fabric guides, you must still test for washability (see p. 16).

If the clothes pass the test, use the following stain removal methods before you wash the garment. Because most old fabrics are fragile, the best first step in stain removal is to soak the material in lukewarm water for about 20 minutes to make the fibers more pliable. Then follow one of these methods:

Method 1

Soak the clothes in a solution of ¼ cup all-fabric bleach per 2 quarts lukewarm water. Leave about 15 minutes—longer for cotton and linen. Rinse thoroughly. If the fabric seems resilient or the stain is more or less on the surface, go ahead and try one of the other methods, perhaps several if the origin of the stain is unknown.

NOTE: This is an acceptable method for bleaching all but fine lace.

Method 2

For stains that might contain protein—baby formula or fly specks, for example—apply a paste of enzyme pre-soak, rub it in *lightly*, and leave it for 3 or 4 minutes. Then wash out by hand. Reapply if it seems to be working. Rinse very thoroughly.

NOTE: Enzymes can be hard on wool and silk, but they may be the only way to remove a stain. Used sparingly and for only 3 to 5 minutes at a time, they should give good results.

Method 3

To get yellow or brown stains out of *white* cotton or linen, wet the area, then apply a paste of lemon juice and salt to the spot. Tamp it in lightly with a soft brush, then leave to dry in the sun. Rinse. You may be able to whiten brown lace this way if it has first been thoroughly washed and soaked.

- Old brown or yellow age stains are often permanent. It's difficult to trace their origins, but among the possibilities are starch, food, residues of bleach or bluing, rust, and mildew. Almost always, chemical changes have taken place, weakening the fabric—which is why it's unwise to scrub or to chlorine bleach old fabrics. If such stains feel stiff or are powdery when scratched, it's best to leave them alone.
- New stains can generally be removed with the normal methods used on delicate fabrics. See the Stain Chart in Chapter 2.

Cleaning and Washing: By far the most sensible investment, of course, is in clothes that can be washed. Most garments made of wool, silk, or rayon must be *hand*-dry-cleaned in perfectly fresh solvent. Many will need skilled reblocking or re-pressing to get them into shape. This is expensive and requires a fine dry cleaner.

Clothes age as fibers and dyes deteriorate and the inner structure—stitches, lining, etc.—gives way. The finish that gave yarns resilience, body, and even texture also deteriorates with time. So if you can wash the item, go gently. Before you go ahead, be sure to remove lace, ribbon, and any other trim so that you can treat it separately. Most old metal hooks and buttons aren't rust-proof, so take them off, too.

To care for clothes, you won't need any special equipment and supplies other than a net sweater dryer and a square of nylon mesh from the dimestore which you should cut to about 8 inches by 8 inches, binding the edges with masking tape. Be sure you have the ordinary laundry supplies plus baking soda, distilled water, liquid castile soap, all-fabric bleach, and perhaps washing soda.

Method 1

This is for clothes that are essentially clean but need perking up. Let cotton and linen soak for an hour—washable wool, silk, or rayon for only 20 minutes—in a solution of 1 tablespoon of baking soda per 1 quart distilled water. Remove clothes immediately if color starts to bleed; roll between two towels. This will stop the bleeding. Turn problem clothes over to a specialist.

If the clothes respond well, rinse gently and roll between towels to extract water. Repeat the process once or twice if needed.

Method 2

This is for dirtier fabrics. It also revives color in many fabrics. Make a solution of 1 tablespoon of baking soda and ¼ cup of hot water. Add 1 gallon of distilled water and make suds, using castile soap or a specialty textile soap.* Soak the clothes as in Method 1, but for only half the time allowed. To the *second-to-the-last* rinse add 1 tablespoon of white vinegar per 1 gallon of cool water.

Method 3

This is specifically for damask and other old linens. Soak them for several hours in a solution of ¼ cup of borax per 1 gallon of warm water. Stir occasionally and change the solution when it looks dirty. The next step is to rinse, then soak a further half hour or so in a solution of 1 tablespoon of soap or detergent and 1 tablespoon of washing soda per 1 gallon of warm water. Rinse again, then launder, using fresh soap or detergent. For truly bright whites and a lovely fresh smell, stretch the linens flat and dry them in the sun.

Linen should be ironed while quite damp, but if it has softened with age you may need to let it dry and use spray starch to crisp it up.

Method 4

This is an old-fashioned but still extremely successful way to whiten or brighten *all* whites and colors. Use it only with sturdy cotton or linen, however. It is excellent for today's clothes, too—children's grimy shirts and socks, for example. It even works on some polycottons.

Bring a *large* pot of water to a slow boil, adding a tablespoon or so of borax to soften it, if necessary. There should be enough water so the clothes float freely. Stir in 2 tablespoons of soap flakes or castile soap per 1 gallon of water. Submerge one or two items at a time in the suds, stirring them for about five minutes. Lift out with tongs and check on progress once or twice. *Do not leave clothes unattended, as air trapped under them can cause boil-over.*

*Procter & Gamble make Orvus WA; Lever Brothers, D. W. 300; and GAF Corporation, Igepal. Museums can direct you to a source or call these companies.

If the clothes still look dingy, add another tablespoon of soap. (You can add 1 tablespoon of chlorine bleach if the clothes are in good condition.) Continue stirring.

After a few minutes, remove the clothes and rinse in cool water; an alternative is to put the pot under a faucet and simply run water in until the clothes are cool and no soap remains.

Since old yarns and fabrics aren't nearly as resilient as newer ones, it's a good idea to lay them flat to dry, pulling and smoothing gently to shape.

The basic rule is *don't iron* vintage clothes, as long as you can make them presentable by simply steaming them. If you must iron, use the lowest practical setting and work on the reverse, or protect the face of the fabric with a presscloth. NOTE: For glossy linen you will have to iron it directly on the face.

To stiffen old fabrics, try spray-on sizing first. If that's not sufficient, use dried or liquid starch following package directions. *Sheer* cotton, linen, and silk can be given a light stiffening by dipping them in a cooled solution of 1 teaspoon of borax per 1 quart of warm water. Let dry until damp, then iron.

Old fibers crease more easily and may even break at folds, so be careful when folding garments for storage. Thin fabrics have a pronounced tendency to droop if they are not stored flat and stuffed to shape with tissue paper.

Follow the regular storage guidelines in Chapter 6, but also:

- Use plenty of tissue paper—the acid-free type mentioned in Chapter 6, if possible.
- Be sure to allow for some air circulation—padding with tissue helps. If you live in an area of heavy pollution, be sure to cover well. *Never* let clothes come in contact with wood or paint, as chemicals can be harmful.
- Try to maintain a steady temperature, in the neighborhood of 65° F., and keep humidity down while avoiding a very dry atmosphere.
- Take out and brush or shake out every six months or so. Be sure to change folds to keep marks from setting.
- Dust can work its way into thick wools. To get it out, lay the garment flat, place the nylon mesh square on top, and using the upholstery attachment of the vacuum on low suction, go over the whole garment, moving the mesh as necessary.

To reduce strain on wet, weak fibers, drain and refill the sink or tub to rinse rather than lifting the clothes out. If you think something might stretch too much when wet, lay it on a net sweater dryer in the bathtub to do the cleaning—just sponge suds through it to wash, then rinse by pouring water through it. Press water out somewhat, then move the article gently to a dry towel, pat it out flat and to the proper shape, put another towel on top, and roll it up gently but firmly. Repeat with dry towels as necessary.

ALL ABOUT DYEING ————————————

Do you want to brighten up a thrift-shop find, or rescue a much-loved but faded piece of clothing? Fabric dyeing can be the answer. The national brands of dye available at dimestores and sewing supply shops give perfectly satisfactory results and are easy to use.

Use the Dyeing Chart to zero in on fibers that will dye well. Follow the standard package directions for the stove-top method, but supplement them with the Dyeing Guidelines below.

You will need a 4-gallon enameled or stainless steel pot (perhaps bigger for large items), a long-handled stainless steel or wooden spoon, a pair of tongs, rubber gloves, a scale for weighing the clothes, dye, and if you're stripping out old color, color remover. (It is sold along with dyes. Be sure to get the amount prescribed for the dry weight of the clothes.)

NOTE: To make matching thread, wind a sufficient amount of white cotton—or cotton-wrapped polyester—thread around a spoon handle and use it to stir while the clothes are dyeing.

STEP-BY-STEP DYEING GUIDELINES

1. Weigh the clothes *dry* before you buy the dye. Ordinarily you need one package of dye per pound, but consult the Dyeing Chart. Generally you use less to get pastels, more to dye heavy materials or to get deeper tones or when dyeing at lower temperatures.

2. Wash out all possible stains. If the clothes are clean, presoak them 15 minutes in water to swell the fibers and make them more receptive to the dye. (Don't expect dyes to "take" as well as they do on new clothes.)

3. There are a number of standard colors, but to get more varied shades, try one of the following recipes*:
    Per Pound Standard Fabric
    Terra Cotta: 1 package of tan/1 package of coral
    Flesh: 2 teaspoons of tan/1 teaspoon of pink
    Ecru: 2 teaspoons of tan/1 teaspoon of orange
    Denim: 1 package of navy blue/½ package of aqua
    Cranberry: 1 package of scarlet/½ package of wine red
    Midnight Blue: 2 packages of navy/½ package of black

*These and the "dyeing over" suggestions are adapted from material provided by RIT, Inc.

Ivory: 1 teaspoon of tan/½ teaspoon of yellow
Emerald Green: 1 package of jade green/1 package of kelly green
Lime Green: 1 package of yellow/1 package of light green
Burgundy: 1 package of wine red/1 package of bright (cardinal) red

You can also dye over existing color, but the results are somewhat unpredictable, as they depend not only on the original dye and the fiber being dyed but on the condition of the fabric. (Dyeing over a pattern is most difficult. For best results, choose the darkest shade that predominates in the print.)

IF YOU DYE	WITH	YOU GET
Bright yellow	Red	Deep orange
Red	Blue	Purple
Light blue	Pink	Lavender
Yellow	Blue	Green
Medium brown	Green	Olive
Green	Blue	Aqua
Purple	Navy	Plum
Orange	Tan	Burnt orange
Tan	Rose pink	Dusty rose
Red or wine	½ package dark green	Black
Green	½ package scarlet	Black
Brown	½ package navy blue	Black

4. Old clothes should be dyed at no more than 130° F. unless they are very sturdy cotton or linen. Extend dyeing time as necessary to get deeper colors. A candy thermometer will keep track of the temperature.

5. Optional: When dyeing, add 1 tablespoon of salt to the dye bath, as it helps transfer dye from the water to the fibers.

6. To prevent streaking, stir continuously and keep the temperature of the dye bath as steady as possible.

7. If the color is too light when the article has dried, you can dye it again, provided the clothes reacted well the first time.

8. Rinse clothes first in warm water, then in gradually cooler water to remove all extra dye.

9. To be sure you get an even tone, roll freshly dyed clothes between two towels. *Do not wring or squeeze.* Spread them to dry on fresh, old dry towels, making sure they are flat and turning them several times during drying. Do not dry in direct sun or the color may fade.

10. Iron damp or dry according to the fabric. Colors will stay brighter if you iron on the back of the material.

11. Dyed clothes should always be washed separately or with clothes of similar color. Instead of tackling

DYEING CHART (INCLUDES DYEABLE FIBERS ONLY)

	SPECIAL NOTES	COLOR REMOVER	DYEING TEMPERATURE (DEGREES F.)
Acetate	Difficult to dye; heat can damage.	No	130°–160°
Cotton		Yes; 160°F	160°–180°
Linen	Can be hard to dye.	Yes; 140°F	160°–180°
Nylon	Won't dye deep color.	Yes; 140°F	140°
Rayon	Difficult to dye; heat can damage.	No	130°–160°
Silk	Difficult to dye; heat can damage; dye only white or ecru	No	130°
Wool	Won't dye deep color.	No	130°

stains with hot water, bleach, or enzyme presoaks, use plain soap, mild detergent, or a laundry bar soap.
12. To clean the dyeing pot, scrub with scouring powder (any household cleanser containing bleach).

Some typical weights: Woman's wool sweater: ½ pound. Man's ribbed fisherman's sweater: one pound. Pair of cotton twill pants: one pound. Woman's light cotton dress: one pound. Heavier cotton (denim) dress shirt or circular (full) skirt: two pounds.

AMOUNT OF DYE	RECOMMENDED TIME
1½ the usual amount	Standard time
Standard*	Standard time
Standard	Standard time; longer for deep tones
½ the usual amount	½ the standard time
Standard	¾ the standard time
Standard	20–30 minutes
1½ the usual amount	20–30 minutes

*The standard amount of dye to use—unless otherwise indicated—is one package per pound of clothing.

CHAPTER TWELVE

Fibers and Fabrics from A to Z

Knowing the difference between fibers and fabrics is a basic step in handling clothes confidently. *Fibers* make up the yarns of which the fabric is woven. Their characteristics determine the basic care the article of clothing needs.

Fabrics are defined by the *way* yarns have been woven or knitted and perhaps finished. This also affects care (for example, a honan silk is usually washable, while a silk brocade isn't).

Look up the fiber first. The entry will tell you such things as which cleaning agents are safe and what ironing method is generally best. Then check the fabric name—say, crepe, chiffon, or gabardine—for specific tips. For washing, refer to the Chart on p. 68.

THE FIBERS

ACETATE:

Colorfast, wrinkle-resistant, firmly woven, and comfortable in warm or cool weather. Resists perspiration damage.

Disadvantages: Doesn't have much give. Isn't for active wear.

Care: *Dry Cleaning:* Most acetates require dry cleaning. But see labels. *Spot Removal: Do not spot clean unless washable,* and turn to the dry cleaner if the standard home stain-removal methods require acetone, alcohol, ammonia, amyl acetate (banana oil), chlorine bleach, or trichloroethylene cleaning fluid, or if the stain is old. *Washing:* Handwash washables separately—they may not be entirely colorfast. If label says machine-dryable, use only a low setting (acetate dries quickly) and remove while still faintly damp. Otherwise, dry flat. *Ironing:* Steam iron on low Permanent Press setting and lower heat if the iron sticks at all, as acetate melts at over 300° F. Do touch-ups on a steam setting.

ACRYLIC/MODACRYLIC:

Inexpensive, no-iron wool substitutes. Colorfast and soft; resists damage from light and acids like perspiration. *Disadvantages:* Both pill badly, especially in knits and napped wovens, and both attract dirt, collect lint and static, and have a short life. They are also more sensitive to heat than other man-mades; machine drying too long can ruin them, as can ironing at higher than low Permanent Press setting.

Care: *Dry Cleaning:* Does not dry clean well, but knit outerwear with modacrylic pile (fleece) trim or lining must be dry cleaned. *Spot Removal:* You can use all cleaning agents *except* acetone, alcohol, and dry-cleaning fluid. *Washing:* Do by hand or on a Permanent Press or Gentle/Knit cycle with warm or cold water wash, cold rinse, and a detergent. Turning inside out will reduce pilling and linting. *Drying:* Use only low settings and run for no more than 10 minutes before checking. Remove when barely dry. If you don't want to wait and check the dryer, hang up to air-dry instead. *Ironing:* If you have to iron, use the lowest possible steam setting. You can sometimes fluff *dry* matted pile with a carding or dog comb, but work slowly and carefully.

COTTON:

Good quality is naturally absorbent, washable, resists wrinkling, irons easily, shrinks minimally, and is comfortable in hot weather. Add 8 to 18 percent polyester, and cotton is perfect for active wear. Look for tags that say Sanforized or preshrunk or mercerized, which add strength and smoothness as well as shrink resistance, and SuPima, the sign of the fine, long-staple cotton backed by the SuPima marketing association. Knits are no-iron. *Disadvantages:* Low-grade cotton degrades quickly, wrinkles easily, and shrinks unpredictably. Assume one size shrinkage for most cottons unless marked preshrunk or Sanforized. Allow for up to 5 inches of shrinkage in pants during machine washing and drying.

(Denim, chino, corduroy, flannel, knits, and loose weaves shrink most.)

Care: *Dry Cleaning:* Cotton dry cleans reasonably well, but washing revives and refreshes it. You *must* wash handpainted and pigment-printed clothes. *Spot Removal:* Colorfast cotton with no durable-press finish should come clean easily. *Washing:* Cotton will last much longer if presoaked when very dirty, washed gently, *without chlorine bleach*, and air rather than machine dried. If you want to prevent or minimize shrinkage, wash gently in cool water and then line dry. *Drying:* Dry inside out to slow fading and wear. To soften line-dried cottons such as towels, tumble dry on a low or No Heat setting a few minutes before hanging them up. *Ironing:* Cotton without durable press must be damp to iron up smooth and crisp. Spray-on sizing may be used on dry fabric. (Since there are so many cotton fabrics, look up the name of the fabric for specific recommendations.) To touch up, try steam ironing or spray with sizing and iron dry.

NOTE: As you gain experience, you will sometimes be able to ignore "Dry Clean Only" labels on cotton, but *never* machine dry these cottons. Use the washability test on p. 16 before taking the plunge, and *always* dry clean the first few times.

DURABLE PRESS:

Manufacturers use two kinds of durable-press treatments: resin or a liquid ammonia. Both relax fibers so they don't wrinkle, don't shrink, and can be machine dried on Permanent Press. Resin finishes add body. Ammonia treatment leaves clothes feeling like cotton. *Disadvantages:* Resins give a synthetic feel and wear off after about fifty washings, leaving the fabric limp and raggy. Neither treatment releases stains easily. When buying, avoid anything that feels stiff or has a fishy odor, as these are defective.

Care: *Dry Cleaning:* Like the synthetics, durable press doesn't dry clean well. *Spot Removal:* Treat as polyester if a polyblend; 100 percent cotton as cotton. Though labels usually say "No Bleach," you *can* use chlorine bleach when all else fails. Rinse *thoroughly*, however. *Washing:* Treat polyblends as polyester; 100 percent cotton as cotton. If the clothes have pleats, turn them inside out during machine washing and use only a Gentle/Knit cycle. Even better, remove them before the final spin and hang to drip dry, pinned evenly across the top of the pleats. *Ironing:* Some durable-press items will need light ironing to look their best. Use a Permanent Press or medium steam setting. *Never use a hot iron* because it will yellow resins. 100 percent cotton may need some spray-on sizing to give it a crisp finish. Touch up by steam ironing.

LINEN:

Linen yarns come from the flax plant. Good quality is smooth, durable, crisp-textured, and cool-wearing. It is naturally lint-free, shrinks minimally (unless loosely woven), can take all cleaning agents as long as it's colorfast, can be sterilized by boiling, and usually irons up crisp and glossy without starching. When buying, look for fabric that is firmly woven, has a full, crisp feel (hand), and is marked "Pure Linen" (or "100% Linen" or "All Linen"). (Cotton linen is *cotton* with a linen weave.) Labels that say 'Mercerized' or vat-dyed labels assure you that the article is colorfast. *Disadvantages:* Linen wrinkles, often because it is so loosely woven. It can also fray and unravel at cut edges unless these are pinked, bound, hemmed, or protected by a lining.

Care: *Dry Cleaning:* Dry clean only when necessary. Whites and pastels should be entrusted only to a cleaner who changes the solvent often and takes the trouble to do light clothes as a separate load. *Spot Removal:* Linen responds well to spot cleaning as long as it's *colorfast.* Check before you go to work. Proceed as for cotton, when applicable, or durable press. *Washing:* In general, treat as cotton, but don't leave colors to soak, as dyes may loosen. Wash colors separately, and don't wring or twist or put in a regular laundry load, since the fibers, though strong, can be brittle. *Drying: Never machine dry.* Only whites should be dried in the sun; colors would fade. Pull to shape gently but firmly while drying to make ironing easier. Thin fabric will be ready for ironing in about half an hour. *Ironing:* As for cotton, but since linen has stiffer, longer fibers, *wet* it evenly at the start of ironing to get crisp results. For a good, flat finish, work on the reverse side with a presscloth, using a Cotton setting. Do the same when working on seams, zippers, and other ridges. (Use Linen setting only if the lower setting doesn't give good results.) Be careful not to overiron, as linen scorches easily. Press pleats and hems down gently. To do a touch-up, try steam ironing; alternatively you can lay a damp cloth over wrinkles, press, then remove the cloth and finish pressing.

NOTE: White linen, free from stains, can be dyed. To revive faded color, rinse in water to which a tablespoon or two of vinegar has been added.

NYLON:

Strong, elastic, and abrasion-resistant, nylon washes easily. An extremely versatile fiber, running the gamut from stockings to Velcro closings. *Disadvantages:* Often pills badly and doesn't allow air to pass through, trapping moisture. Picks up soil and color easily in washing. When buying, look for no-iron, colorfast materials. Knits—as in tights—may shrink, so buy one size larger than normal unless you will handwash them. Make sure the lining or backing in nylon clothes is nylon.

Care: *Dry Cleaning:* Nylon doesn't dry clean well. If you must dry clean, ask that it be kept separate from very dirty or dark-colored items and that it be pressed only on the original creases. Otherwise you will have *two* permanent creases. *Stain Removal:* You can use any cleaning agent, even chlorine bleach if all else fails. As nylon attracts oily dirt, you'll want to have a grease solvent handy. *Washing:* In general, nylon must be washed often to keep stains from setting. Turn inside out for machine washing, use detergent. Don't use hot temperature, and *be sure to keep white and pastels separate from dark or bright colors or trim that might bleed. Drying:* Nylon is quick-drying. Especially if pleated, it will look better and last a lot longer if hung up to dry. Do not hang in direct sun. If you do machine dry, check after 10 minutes, and remove the minute it is dry. *Ironing:* If it's needed, use a low steam setting (medium for Quiana). Can be touched up by steam ironing. If knit, try running in the dryer on low heat with a damp towel for a few minutes to remove wrinkles.

OLEFIN:

A plastic fiber used in papery nonwoven fabric but also blended into knit socks, sportswear, and underwear. Extremely lightweight but warm; weatherproof but also comfortable in warm weather; sturdy and stain resistant. Is colorfast and won't shrink unless exposed to heat. *Disadvantages:* A papery feel, lack of give in wear, a mussed look because it can't be ironed. Oily stains can become permanent as well.

Care: *Dry Cleaning:* Olefin can't be dry cleaned. *Spot*

Removal: If tackled promptly, many spots wipe off with soap and water. *Washing:* Follow label directions or handwash gently in cool water with any detergent. Don't wring or twist, just slosh around. Press water out gently, pull to shape as smoothly as possible, and hang or dry flat. Do not iron.

POLYESTER:

The most durable fiber of the man-mades. When it is made up into fabric, durability varies. Can be given permanent pleats set in by the manufacturer. Is wrinkle- and shrink-resistant, and in concentrations of over 8 percent in blends will prevent shrinkage of cotton and rayon. Some polyester fabrics have pill-, static-, or abrasion-resistant finishes as a bonus. *Disadvantages:* Stains easily, and in some fabrics pills. Anything with more than 35 percent polyester can be uncomfortable to wear, as it doesn't breathe.

Care: *Dry Cleaning:* Polyester doesn't always dry clean well, so as a practical matter buy washable polyester. If you do dry clean, review the notes under nylon. *Spot Removal:* Treat as nylon unless in a high cotton-content blend, in which case treat as cotton. Ditto rayon blends. Be sure to pretest *blends* for colorfastness. Water-based stains are usually easy to remove. *Washing:* Polyester and polycottons are *the* fabrics for the Permanent Press washer and dryer cycle. Use cold or warm water and detergent. *Handwash* thin, silky polyesters. *Drying:* The Permanent Press cycle is ideal, but remove as soon as the clothes are dry or the permanent-press can be damaged. If you have only a choice between Heat and No-Heat, run polyester until nearly dry on Heat, then on No-Heat for about 10 minutes. Remove promptly to prevent crumpling. *Ironing:* If needed, use a low to medium steam setting. Higher temperatures can fuse the fiber, leaving a permanent mark. Touch up with steam.

RAMIE:

A linen-like fiber, usually found as a small percentage of a cotton, rayon, or acrylic blend. It is lustrous and dyes well. Blended with cotton, it adds strength. *Disadvantages:* Ramie can feel stiff and scratchy. Rayon or acrylic blended with ramie are less long-lasting, as the stiffer ramie frays the softer fibers.

Care: Ramie should be treated as the other fibers in the blend or as linen. Because it is brittle, take care not to iron in creases, as they may not come out.

RAYON:

Sometimes called a semi-synthetic because unlike true synthetics, which are petroleum-based, rayon is made from waste cotton or other plant material. Its care is closer to that of cotton. Less expensive than silk. Adds softness in blends with stiffer fabrics. *Disadvantages:* Not nearly as durable as cotton or linen. Often not washable because it weakens when wet and stretches or shrinks out of shape. Tends to droop rather quickly and very little is good quality, though trademarked brands and European rayon blends are more reliable. May not be colorfast, wrinkles, is confining and clammy in hot weather because it doesn't breathe like cotton, and picks up dirt easily, especially if the fabric is nubby. Since it soils easily, "Dry Clean Only" rayon can be expensive to maintain. Also called "viscose".

Care: *Dry Cleaning:* Rayon dry cleans well, and as indicated, most must be dry cleaned. (However, vintage rayon lingerie can be handwashed and pressed when damp-dry.) A number of today's trademarked rayons are washable, and the label will say so. *Spot Removal:* Try home methods only if the clothes are washable and colorfast. Exception: Flush perspiration out with a little water before dry cleaning. (Treat as a delicate fabric.) *Washing:* Handwash. White rayon can be bleached as a last resort to brighten it, but use a *mild* chlorine bleach solution. *Drying:* To prevent sagging, dry flat. *Ironing:* Iron on a Permanent Press or Wool setting while just slightly damp. Avoid stretching and adding shine by ironing with a light hand on the wrong side. To touch up, use a steam setting.

SILK:

Most silk cloth is made of cultivated silk fiber, which is not coarse and crisp like wild silk, though both have been processed, removing some of the natural gum coating. (Raw silk has not been processed and many people are allergic to it.) As with other natural fibers, different fabrics have different advantages. Silk is naturally wrinkle-resistant, though low-grade silks wrinkle badly. High-quality silk sheds wrinkles with a little steaming, doesn't shrink, and can go a number of wearings between cleanings because it sheds dirt. Silk should feel full in the hand except for thin, crisp fabrics like organza. Fluid silks should feel creamy. Be sure to find out the name of the fabric, since this is the key to proper care. Good silk will last for years if properly cared for. Beware of handpainted silks, however, as colors often will not hold. *Disadvantages:* Silk dyes travel when affected by substances like perspiration, and damage is permanent. Silk is also inelastic and will split and fray if clothes fit too tightly. White silk yellows in time, especially in the sun, and can't be rewhitened. Cut edges ravel; seams and hems *must* be finished neatly, adding to the cost.

Care: *Dry Cleaning:* Dry clean all deep colors, prints, and blends with wool, cotton, or rayon and clothes with a pressed-in design such as pleats, since it isn't permanent. Otherwise dry clean or wash according to the fabric guide, which lists each silk fabric. Cleaning should be done about every three or four wearings (as soon as possible if you perspire or stain clothes) because bacteria from the body create ammonia, which attacks silk fiber and some dyes. Caution: Dry clean *all silk* the first few times it gets dirty, then consider whether it's washable. *Washing:* Handwash silk gently if (1) it passes the washability test on page 16, (2) the clothes aren't on the "Dry Clean Only" list in Chapter 5, and (3) the fabric is listed as washable in the fabric guide. Work quickly. If you misjudge and color starts to run, drain the sink, rinse the garment quickly in cool water, then put between *two* towels and roll to extract water. To keep whites white, add a drop or two of ammonia to the suds. After rinsing, roll in a towel until ready to iron. To keep pale colors bright, add 1 or 2 tablespoons of vinegar to the second-to-the-last rinse. *Stain Removal:* Stains on garments labeled "Dry Clean Only" *must* be handled by a cleaner. Turn over even washable silk to the cleaner *unless* the stain comes out with dry-cleaning fluid or washes out with mild soap and water—glycerin is okay, too. Treat stains promptly so they can't set. When using cleaning fluid, be sure to feather out the liquid over a large area to avoid rings. Dry with a hairdryer held about 6 inches from the fabric and set on low heat and low speed. In general, try to work up and down, parallel to the warp threads instead of crosswise. As perspiration is so harmful, flush it out with a little water to which a few *drops* of ammonia have been added as soon as possible. Then rinse. If the clothes must be dry cleaned, alert the cleaner to deal with areas of perspiration. *Drying: Never* machine dry. Thin silks are often dry enough for ironing after half an hour or so. *Ironing:* Silk must be *evenly* damp or it will not iron smooth. Use only low settings and iron or press on the reverse to preserve colors or use a thin presscloth on the face. You can do a quick touch-up with a steam iron on the face or the back. (Use only a cool, dry iron on the back to touch-up taffeta, organza, moiré, faille, and embossed silk to prevent water spotting.) *As silk is elastic, don't pull the fabric while ironing because you will end up with puckers.*

SPANDEX:

An elastic form of polyurethane now used instead of rubber fibers because it resists chemicals such as swimming pool chlorine, perspiration, and suntan oil better, lasts longer, and is dyeable. Brand-name spandex is your best bet. *Disadvantages:* Not long-wearing and thus shortens the life of clothes containing other, more durable fibers. If it has not been properly used it pops out, showing as little loops on the surface of bathing suits, for example.

Care: *Dry Cleaning:* Spandex does not dry clean well. *Spot Removal:* Treat as the covering fiber—nylon, for example—but avoid where possible bleach, amyl acetate, coconut oil, and dry-cleaning fluid. Laundry bar soap is good for removing oily spots. *Washing:* Wash as for the predominant fiber in the blend, but do not subject to hot water or long drying. When spandex is present in larger amounts, say in swimwear, it's recommended that you simply rinse it in cool or lukewarm water and gently squeeze dry. To get out soil, use only soap flakes or dishwashing liquid or detergent. *Drying:* Pull gently to shape, dry flat, and *never* dry in the sun. Avoid machine drying where possible. If necessary use a low setting for 10 minutes or so.

TRIACETATE:

A sturdier form of acetate, even more wrinkle-resistant and washable. Does not pill or shrink. Very successful as an inexpensive substitute for crisp silks and in blends. Brand-name acetates and European imports offer the most reliable quality. Look for "Static-Resistant Finish" on clothes tags. *Disadvantages:* Not long-wearing, confining in warm weather, and cannot be let out, as the original seam or hem marks will show.

Care: *Dry Cleaning:* Follow label instructions, as triacetate can be either washed or dry cleaned. *Stain Removal:* As for acetate. Do not rub or wring. If label says machine-washable, remove clothes before the final spin to cut down on wrinkling, then drip dry. To help knits dry to shape, slip a towel *inside,* smooth to shape, and sandwich between two more towels. *Ironing:* Steam iron on a medium setting or iron while slightly damp. See Acetate for further information.

WOOL:

Commonly refers to sheep's fleece but also to lamb's wool and the specialty wools (hair) of Angora rabbit and goat, cashmere goat, camel, alpaca, vicuna, and qiviut (musk ox). Warm, won't shrink if dry cleaned or handwashed gently, can be worn a number of times between cleanings because (1) it sheds dirt in many cases and (2) it's resilient. Tweeds and worsteds, especially if twilled, like gabardine, are very durable. Easy to alter because the old seam and hem marks can be steamed and pressed out. Specialty wools are finer, smoother, longer wearing, and less likely to pill—except for Angora rabbit. When buying, look for a full, supple hang, fabric that sheds wrinkles easily, very elastic ribbing in knits, and a lining in soft woolen fabrics. Unless cashmere is two- or three-ply, is fully fashioned (that is, each piece of the pattern is knit separately), and has excellent elasticity in the ribbing at collar, cuffs, *and* waist, it is not worth present extravagant prices. Look for clear colors with no dark hairs, too. *Disadvantages:* If sheep or lamb's wool and some specialty wools are not handwashed gently in cool water, they will shrink and mat—permanently. Only wools so labeled can be machine washed. See Chapter 7 for how to remove pills.

Care: *Dry Cleaning:* All wools must be dry cleaned except for the standard knits, those that pass the washability test, and the washable wools. For proper maintenance, see Chapter 6. *Stain Removal:* Wools don't soak things up quickly. You can often get most of a stain out if you blot promptly and thoroughly. After emergency action, take Wools labeled "Dry Clean Only" to the cleaner. Because wool is sensitive to many chemicals you should not use home methods that require:

acetone	ammonia (except as below under "Special Treatment")	enzymes (except as directed on the Stain Chart)
alcohol (except diluted with 10 parts water)	chlorine bleach	a hard-surface household cleaner
regular laundry detergents	color remover	

When spot cleaning, sponge or blot *with the warp threads,* not crosswise. *Washing:* Handwash unless labeled "Machine Wash." The wools that are likely to be washable are knits, blankets, and fine flat-woven scarves. To prevent felting, never rub, never use warm or hot water, never leave clothes to soak more than 15 minutes—three minutes is enough for normal cleaning. Always rinse gently but well, since residues of cleaning agents are especially hard on wool. Always use soap flakes or dishwashing liquid. Always wash whites separately, using 1 teaspoon of all-fabric bleach (and 1 tablespoon of borax if the water is hard) per quart of wash water to keep them white. You can try bluing, too. *Drying:* Do not machine dry unless the label says to. Never dry in direct sun or near a heat source. Wools need to retain a little moisture to be at their best.

Special Treatments:

1. To renew suppleness, put a few drops of olive oil or glycerin in the rinse water.
2. To bring up color, put 1 teaspoon of ammonia in the next-to-the-last rinse, then rinse again using 1 teaspoon of vinegar in the water.
3. To restore crushed nap, steam the clothes well. While the fibers are damp *but not wet,* brush against the nap very lightly with a soft brush. On sturdy tweeds use a wire dog comb, being careful not to dig into the underlying fabric.
4. To reblock knits, soak a bit in lukewarm water in which a tablespoon of baking soda has been dissolved. Rinse. Press out water and shape flat to the dimensions you wish. Pin the article in place if need be. (But take jersey knits to a good cleaner to reblock.)
5. To get lint, cat hairs, and fluff off, use the upholstery attachment of the vacuum on low to medium suction. At the same time brush with a medium-stiff brush. *Ironing:* Knits should not need ironing, but if they do, put face down on a press pad and press lightly. Let steam do most of the work. With other wools try hanging up and steaming first. This is especially handy when traveling. Gently shape and smooth by hand—clothes must be hanging up. If this doesn't work, iron, or rather *press,* since you want to avoid shine. Let steam from the iron penetrate well between each pressure of the iron, which should be on a wool-steam

setting. A well-padded board is *essential* for good results. Don't press until bone-dry. Instead, leave in position for 10 seconds, fanning to evaporate the last
moisture. Then hang up and air to set the press before putting the garment away. To reshape rounded
areas, stuff with a rolled towel or do on the sleeveboard. Let steam penetrate well, then press lightly.

THE FABRICS ————————————

ANGORA: A fine wool made from the hair of the Angora
rabbit or the Angora goat. Angora from a rabbit is fragile,
short-lived, and mats easily, so dry clean or use the
handwashing method for long-haired fabric in Chapter
3. Angora from a goat handwashes nicely.

BASTISTE: Light, sheer, plain weave in mercerized cotton, silk, wool, or man-mades. Handwash cotton, silk
and blends. Dry clean wool.

BOUCLÉ: A fabric that can be made of either wool or
synthetics. Has surface curls. Picks up dirt easily; clean
before dirt gets embedded. If washable, *hand*wash.

BROADCLOTH: A fine, fairly lustrous, tightly woven
cotton, silk, wool, or man-made fabric with a horizontal
rib and sometimes a slight nap. Dry clean wool. Handwash or dry clean silk. Wash cotton and man-mades.

BROCADE: Thick jacquard weave, often with a raised
pattern. Dry clean silk and gold brocade. Leave stain removal to the dry cleaner. Handwash or dry clean other
fibers.

BRUSHED NYLON: Best quality is 100 percent nylon
with *uncut* loops; as they don't pill as sheared loops do.
Use only Gentle/Knit machine cycle and turn inside out
to wash.

CHALLIS: Soft, napped cotton, silk-wool, wool, or
rayon fabric. Dry clean wool and silk-wool blend. Handwash others. Steam-iron face down.

CHARMEUSE: Silk, polyester, and blends in a soft,
shiny fabric. Dry clean silk. Handwash others very
gently. Be careful to iron flat, pinning slippery material
before ironing and working only in the warp direction
and not crosswise. To touch up silk, steam iron on the
reverse.

CHEESECLOTH: A gauze. Use cotton, not nylon, for
clothes care.

CHENILLE: See Bouclé.

CHIFFON: Now made in synthetics as well as silk. Dry clean silk and man-mades. Let the dry cleaner deal with stains. See charmeuse for ironing directions.

CHINCHILLA CLOTH: Dry clean this nubby cloth regularly, whatever the fiber used. If not cleaned, often will deteriorate quickly.

CHINO: Cotton or polycotton in firm weave. Best is mercerized, preshrunk cotton or polycotton with less than 18 percent polyester. Wash or dry clean.

CHINTZ: Printed, slightly glossy cotton, man-made or blend. Modern chintzes have a permanent finish so they can be machine washed on Gentle/Knit cycle, but remove before spin and hang neatly to drip dry. Handwash old chintz and then starch. Iron while damp on the right side for gloss.

CIRÉ: Dry clean this treated cloth unless labeled washable. Take to the dry cleaner to deal with stains. Iron on reverse.

CLOQUÉ: Dry clean cotton and silk. Let the dry cleaner deal with stains. Iron on reverse.

CORDUROY: Can be cotton, or polycotton plush or low-pile wales. Best performer is cotton with small percent polyester and a twill ground. Cotton will shrink *at least* 4 percent. Launder for soft feel; otherwise dry clean. Iron face down on a well-padded board using steam.

CREPE: Silk and wool crepe must be dry cleaned. With synthetics, follow label directions. Iron on reverse.

CREPE DE CHINE: Silk and man-made smooth, somewhat shiny fabric. Handwash silk if it passes the washability test, but take to the dry cleaner if stained. Handwash or dry clean man-mades.

CRINKLE COTTON AND SILK: Handwash. Wring out gently. Hang to dry. When fairly dry, twist handfuls then pull gently to shape working from top to bottom. Do not iron. If you dry clean, tell cleaner you want crinkles left in.

CUPRO: Rayon (51%)-Cotton (49%) blend. Treat as rayon/delicate cotton.

DAMASK: Reversible jacquard. Silk damask must be dry cleaned. Linen should be very firmly woven to be durable. It can be handwashed. Iron on front for gloss.

DENIM: Can be dark-blue twill weave, cotton or polycotton. For durability, cotton with a small percent nylon is best. Heavier weights of 16 ounces, sometimes called workweight or megadenim, last longest. A sign of good quality is that it softens slowly. Cotton shrinks up to 7 percent unless handwashed and hung to dry.

DIMITY: Fine, usually sheer cotton or blend. Handwash.

DOESKIN: Napped cotton or woolen copying real doeskin. Dry clean wool. Handwash cotton.

DOTTED SWISS: The real thing is all cotton with the dots or design sewn on. Handwash. Iron damp. See also flocking.

EYELET: Cotton or man-made. Clip loose threads. When buying, be sure garment it's on is colorfast.

EPONGÉ: Can be wool, rayon, or cotton. Dry clean. Nubby surface attracts dirt, so clean often.

FAILLE: A crosswise rib with crepe or taffeta finish in silk, polyester, and other fibers. Dry clean silk. Handwash or dry clean other versions.

FAKE FUR: Hard-to-clean deep-pile synthetic fibers. Even with careful dry cleaning, may break down. Wipe spills off with cheesecloth dipped in water and wrung out, or in cleaning fluid. Don't press pile down. Hang to dry, then fluff in dryer 1 minute on No Heat setting.

FELT: A wool. Dry clean. To iron, press gently, using steam, on the reverse. Be sure to leave stains to the dry cleaner.

FLANNEL: Cotton, rayon, or wool, napped on both sides. Best are tightly woven and may be twill weave. Dry clean unless baby clothes or a polyblend, which handwash. To iron, steam well, then iron on reverse or with a dry presscloth on top.

FLEECE: Can be wool or man-mades. Dry clean. Leave stains to the dry cleaner.

FLOCKING: Glued-on dots or pattern often removed in dry cleaning. Buy *washable* flocked garments and *hand*wash very gently, using mild soap or detergent.

FOULARD: Plain or twill weave with small print. Dry clean silk and rayon, leaving stains to the dry cleaner. Handwash polyester.

GABARDINE: Durable twill in silk or wool, perhaps with a touch of polyester or nylon. Dry clean. Spots easily. Leave any stains to the dry cleaner. Iron on reverse or with presscloth.

GAUZE: Loose weaves. Dry clean in silk and wool. If cotton, handwash. To return a crinkle effect, after washing take handfuls and wring following warp threads. Then hang to dry. As it dries, pull seams straight to get proper shape.

GEORGETTE: A crepe-finish chiffon. Take silk to cleaner and let him deal with stains. Handwash or dry clean in other fibers. Iron as chiffon.

GINGHAM: Can be cotton or cotton blend. Best is combed cotton. Must be woven of different colored yarns, not simply printed with design. Handwash or machine wash.

GROSGRAIN: Crosswise ribbed silk and other fibers. Dry clean silk and rayon, leaving stains to the dry cleaner. Handwash others unless labeled "Machine wash."

HANDPAINTED FABRICS: Rarely dry clean well. Ask salesperson about care.

HONAN: Nubbed "wild silk" (tussah). Handwash if garment is colorfast and passes washability test.

IRIDESCENT FABRICS: Usually silk. Dry clean and leave all stains to cleaner.

JACQUARD: Repeat design available in many fibers. Dry clean silk, wool, and rayon, leaving all stains to the dry cleaner. To press wool, pin to shape, steam thoroughly, then press.

JERSEY: Plain knit. Dry clean silk or rayon. Leave stains to the dry cleaner. Handwash wool jersey sweaters unless labeled otherwise. Press silk jersey gently on reverse to touch up. Store stuffed with tissue and boxed or in a drawer so it won't stretch out of shape.

LAMÉ: Fabric with real or simulated metallic yarns. Copper and silver tarnish in time and cannot be cleaned. Handwash if simulated metal. Dry clean if silk content. Do not try home stain removal on lamé. Iron on reverse, using low heat, after testing first on seam allowance.

LAWN: A fine, somewhat sheer cotton or blend. Best is combed, preshrunk cotton with a crisp hand. Handwash.

LENO: Lacy-effect fabric in many fibers. Handwash.

LINEN CAMBRIC/HANDKERCHIEF LINEN: Handwash. Starch as needed.

LINEN DAMASK: See damask. Double damask is more durable than single damask and more lustrous. Handwash.

LISLE: Silky cotton knit of long-staple fibers. Must be two or more plies to be durable. Handwash for longer wear.

MACKINAW/MACKINAC: Coarse wool with nap. Dry clean or handwash in warm water with mild soap. Hang to dry, pulling gently to shape as it dries.

MADRAS COTTON: Colors are meant to bleed. Handwash in cold water (but dry clean tailored items).

MARQUISETTE: Can be silk, cotton, and other fibers. Dry clean silk. Handwash or dry clean cotton and others.

MATELASSÉ: Dry clean if silk or if has metallic yarns and leave all stains to the dry cleaner. Others may be handwashed.

MATTE JERSEY: Dry clean no matter what the content and leave all stains to the dry cleaner.

MELTON CLOTH: Thick wool for coats and jackets. Dry clean. Once stains penetrate the nap, take to the dry cleaner.

MOIRÉ: "Watered silk." Dry clean silk, rayon, rayon/acetate, and 100 percent acetate, leaving all stains to the cleaner. Polyester can often be washed. Iron on the reverse with warm, dry iron if "Dry Clean Only." Use steam iron otherwise.

MOUSSELINE: A silk. Dry clean and leave all stains to the dry cleaner.

MUSLIN: Plain-weave cotton or polycotton. Best is combed cotton. Sheets are called muslin if they have 180 thread count per square inch or less. Can be given batiste, chambray, or other finish, and care is determined by finish and garment.

MYLAR™: Handwash. Often wipes clean. Iron on low heat, with steam, on the reverse.

NINON: Smooth, sheer, textured voile. Dry clean silk, rayon, and acetate. Handwash others. Handwash fiberglass (drapes). To touch up, steam iron on the reverse.

NOIL: Spun silk. Dry clean.

NONWOVEN FABRICS: Various fibers held together by heat or chemicals. Should feel firm. Check labels carefully before buying to see if care is practical; many present problems.

ORGANDY: Long-staple sheer cotton with permanent crisp finish. Handwash, then iron damp with dry iron on Wool setting.

ORGANZA: Silk, rayon/acetate, or polyester organdy. Dry clean silk and rayon/acetate, leaving all stains to the dry cleaner. Silk must not get wet or it will water spot. Iron silk with dry iron.

PANNÉ/CRUSHED VELVET: Dry clean if silk. Follow labels otherwise. Iron face down on press pad or towels, steaming well, then pressing *lightly.*

PEAU DE SOIE, PEAU D'ANGE: Silk. Dry clean, leaving all stains to the dry cleaner.

PERCALE: Denser weave than muslin—180 to 240 thread count. Best and really durable is combed, mercerized cotton of 220 thread count or more. Usually cotton or cotton blend. All fibers washable.

PIGMENT-PRINTED FABRIC: A surface printing that will feel stiff on top of the fabric. Do not dry clean—handwash. Not a durable finish.

PIQUÉ: Dimpled fabric with wrinkle-shedding ability but picks up dirt easily. Wonderful in cotton. Handwash unless label directs otherwise.

PLAID: A twilled, worsted wool. Scottish tartan plaids are almost indestructible. Dry clean wool. If refers to pattern, care is determined by fabric.

PLISSÉ: Version of seersucker. Dry clean or do the washability test before trying to wash. Handwash. Iron when *dry.*

POLISHED COTTON: See Chintz.

PONGEE: Light-colored, slubbed "wild silk" (tussah) also copied in cotton and man-mades. Handwash silk if it passes the washability test. If silk, iron while still damp, using a *dry* iron.

POODLECLOTH: Only durable type has loops woven into a woven backing; bonded-on loops come off. Dry clean often to keep clean and leave all stains to the dry cleaner.

POPLIN: Heavy weight of broadcloth in various fibers. Can be waterproofed. Follow label directions to clean. If cotton, hang to dry to prevent shrinkage.

PRINTS: Calicoes, etc. Will stand up to long wear only if dyes have penetrated to the back of the fabric (not just on surface) and are colorfast.

QUILTED FABRICS: Handwash in a tub if natural fiber of same type front, back, and inside. Man-mades should be machine-washable. May be dry cleaned.

REP: Silk or polyester, occasionally blends. Dry clean silk.

SATIN: Can be silk or man-mades. Dry clean silk, leaving all stains to the dry cleaner. Exception: Thin satin lingerie and ribbons can be handwashed. Iron while slightly damp on the reverse. Lightly steam press other satins.

SCHIFFLI EMBROIDERY: Swiss cotton lace on a net backing. Handwash unless on clothes that must be dry cleaned. Press face down on well-padded board.

SEERSUCKER: Built-in puckers that won't wash out. If cotton, handwash, then pull gently to shape and let dry flat or hang up. Machine wash man-mades and blends. Iron lightly face down while damp on a well-padded board.

SERGE: Smooth twill in various weights and fibers. Dry clean, leaving all stains to the dry cleaner. For touch-ups, give soft press with presscloth to avoid shine.

SHANTUNG: Originally a nubby wild silk. Handwash as pongee. Now also copied in cotton and man-mades. Handwash or dry clean as the label indicates.

SHARKSKIN: Wool, silk, and man-mades. Dry clean, leaving all stains to the dry cleaner. To touch up, iron on the reverse or with a presscloth.

SHETLAND: Term loosely used for many soft wools and wool blends. True Shetlands come from Scotland and are wholly or mainly of Shetland Island wool. They are much more durable than the imitations. Handwash sweaters. Dry clean woven wools.

SILK BLENDS: Can be handwashed if other fiber is washable.

SILK LINEN: Linen-weave silk that is handwashable if it passes the washability test.

SLIPPER SATIN: Dry clean and leave all stains to the dry cleaner.

SUEDECLOTH: Suede-finish cloth. Treat as clothes construction and fiber content indicate. Ultrasuede is a washable nonwoven made of polyester.

SURAH: Treat as silk linen.

TAFFETA: Dry clean silk, rayon, and rayon/acetate, leaving all stains to the dry cleaner. Polyester may be washable. Damaged finish on silk can sometimes be re-lustered by a specialty cleaner.

TARTAN: See plaid.

TERRYCLOTH: Only durable and really absorbent if uncut loops on a woven backing in cotton or cotton with a small percent of polyester. Check for a tight weave. Avoid surface-printed designs if you want long wear. Terrycloth should feel like thick toweling.

TRICOT: French for "knitted" and used for a wide variety of knits. Care is determined by fiber. If washable, *hand*wash, as it snaps easily.

TWEED: Should be 100 percent wool for greatest durability. It is naturally stain resistant. Dry clean.

VELOUR: Cut pile in cotton, silk, or synthetics. Dry clean wool or silk velour, leaving all stains to the cleaner. Follow labels for other fibers. Don't iron, simply steam face down on a piece of velvet or corduroy.

VELVET: Pile fabric in various fibers. "Plush" if more than 1/8-inch pile. Blot immediately with cotton towels if it gets wet. Dry clean silk velvet. Do not iron; simply steam while hanging up or put face down on a piece of velvet or corduroy.

VELVETEEN: Low-pile cotton or synthetic velvet. Most practical if designed to be gently machine washed and tumble dried, or hung to dry. To avoid shrinkage in cotton, handwash and hang to dry. If mussed, iron lightly with steam face down or run in the dryer on No Heat or Air Fluff for a few minutes.

VIYELLA™: A British trademark for a 55 percent wool/45 percent cotton twill with a flannel finish. Handwash and iron on the reverse while slightly damp to prevent shine.

VOILE: Now imitated in man-mades but originally a long-staple, sheer, slightly crisp cotton weave. Man-made copies are not comparable. Handwash and iron slightly damp unless nylon or polyester, which can be steam ironed.

WHIPCORD: Wool, cotton, and synthetics. Resembles gabardine. Dry clean wool, leaving all stains to the dry cleaner. Iron on reverse to prevent shine, or use a presscloth.

Index

ABOUT THE AUTHOR

KATHERINE ROBINSON is a journalist with credits ranging from *The Reader's Digest* to *M, The Civilized Man.* She has written straight news and reviews for newspapers in New York City and Connecticut and has a special interest in writing about the practical problems of everyday life. She lives in New York City and has a son and a daughter.

ABOUT THE CONSULTANTS

Necolya Fry has been both a manufacturer and designer of clothing since she graduated from Philadelphia's Drexel University; she currently designs sportswear for the Pacific Clothing Company. She is married and lives on Manhattan's West Side.

Marcia Bayard founded Body Gear, Inc., with Necolya Fry shortly after graduating from Drexel University. She designs sportswear under her own label and for other companies, including Macy's private line of lingerie and at-home wear.

Lara Martina, after a marketing career with Kayser-Roth, has her own line of handknit sweaters. She lives in Stephenville, Newfoundland, with her small daughter, Gallagher.